ANDERS VAN HADEN

ANDERS VAN HADEN

A PICTORIAL BIOGRAPHY

TERRIS C. HOWARD

ANDERS VAN HADEN
A PICTORIAL BIOGRAPHY

iUniverse books may be ordered through booksellers or by contacting:

iUniverse
1663 Liberty Drive
Bloomington, IN 47403
www.iuniverse.com
1-800-Authors (1-800-288-4677)

ISBN: 978-1-5320-5249-1 (sc)
ISBN: 978-1-5320-5250-7 (hc)
ISBN: 978-1-5320-5248-4 (e)

Library of Congress Control Number: 2018907616

Print information available on the last page.

iUniverse rev. date: 07/11/2018

This book is dedicated to Myra Van Haden, wife of Anders Van Haden, who gave me the majority of the material and inspiration for this book.

T.C.H.

Contents

Acknowledgements

I must admit that I cannot take credit for the material presented in this book. I have merely brought together photographs and articles concerning William A. Howard, aka William A. Howell, aka Anders Van Haden. My major contribution to this book was the hours of research and organization of the material in a chronological order.

Myra Van Haden, wife of Anders Van Haden gave three loose-leaf folders containing many original stage and movie stills to Terry and Bill Howard, sons of Charles Clifton Howard, and to Kathy Howell, daughter of William A. Howell, step-brother of Charles Clifton Howard. Many of those stills are in the possession of Terris 'Terry' C. Howard. Movie stills were usually given to the actor as part of his agent's agreement and/or contract with the movie studio or company.

In the course of writing this book, I have benefited from the help of many librarians, authors, experts, actors and actresses. I will try to credit them all by name here.

Ned Comstock, Cinema - TV Library, Doheny Library, University of Southern California for his assistance on researching facts on a Laurel and Hardy movie.

Elizabeth A. Fugate, Drama Library, University of Washington for various approaches to take in my research.

Seattle Public Library, Drama Department for their patience in allowing me to research the Sayre-Carkeek collection.

William G. Smith, Sullivan County Historian, New York for his verification of facts relating to William A. Howell and his daughter, Constance.

Edwin "Ned' Thanhouser, Portland, Oregon, for his cooperation and information on the history and collection of the Thanhouser Company Film Preservation, Inc.

Margaret Herrick Library, Academy of Motion Picture Arts & Sciences, Beverly Hills, California.

UCLA Film and Television Archives, Los Angeles, California.

Brian Tolley, Executive Editor, The Island Packet, Bluffton. South Carolina for permission to use articles from The State newspaper.

Matt Westerhold, Managing Editor, Sandusky Register for permission to use obituary about Anders Van Haden.

Bailey Dabney, The Florence News, Florence, South Carolina for permission to use article about "The Witness Chair."

Hans J. Wollstein, Hoyer, Denmark, for permission to use his article about Anders Van Haden.

Others not mentioned may be credited in the source information.

Acknowledgement is also made to Moon Photo of Seattle, Washington for their excellent custom black and white copy, negative and print work. Also for the wonderful restoration of a silent movie poster.

Permissions

Grateful acknowledgment is made to the following for permission to reprint previously published materials:.

The Author

Terris 'Terry' C. Howard

Terris 'Terry' Clifton Howard was born at the Railroad Hospital, Anchorage, Territory of Alaska. He is the son of Charles Clifton Howard and Hazel Mildred Anderson. Terry retired as a Quality Assurance Manager from The Boeing Company that spanned 42 year. in engineering and quality assurance with The Boeing Company. During his career at The Boeing Company, Terry was assigned to work with Constructiones Aeronauticas, S.A. (CASA) in Sevilla and Madrid, Spain where he met and married Rosa Maria Hidalgo on the 7th of April 1974 in Sevilla, Andalucia, España. His main interest is genealogy and research of his ancestors, the Anderson families of Glen Lednock and the Parish of Comrie, Perthshire, Scotland; the Carmichael families from the Parish of Comrie, Perthshire, Scotland; the Fisher and McCallum families from the Parish of Killin, Perthshire, Scotland.

Terry is a life-time member of the Museum of Flight and was the 727 Crew Chief as a volunteer on the restoration of the first Boeing 727-100, UAL N7001U, at Paine Field, Everett, Washington that flew to the Museum of Flight at Boeing Field on March 2, 2016. Terry can be contacted by email at tch6535@aol.com.

Introduction

This is meant to be a pictorial biographical sketch of Anders Van Haden (aka William Arthur Howard aka William August Howell). William Arthur Howard was my grandfather and I grew up not knowing much about him or his career until his wife Myra Van Haden aroused my interest. What follows is a chronological presentation of known facts on the stage and silent film career of William August Howell, the name used during that era. Following is the stage and motion picture career of Anders Van Haden. I have included pertinent facts that establish the identification of many of the movie stills.

Where possible, programs, reviews, and photographs have been included. Some of the movie stills or candid cast poses from the silent era may be the first time that they ever have been published.

Many of the movie stills that Anders Van Haden had were eventually passed on to his wife, Myra Van Haden. These movie stills were obtained from his agent or the movie studio to be used by his agent or Anders Van Haden. These movie stills are know in the possession These movie stills were usually used in promotion of the actor by his agent or himself in the Standard Casting Directory Listing, various publications the annual Film Daily Year Book of Motion Pictures, etc. Identification of these movie stills is detailed in the Hollywood chapter.

T.C.H.

Seattle
April 2018

FAMILY HISTORY

William Arthur Howard (AKA William August Howell, Anders Van Haden) immigrated to the United States about 1898 from Germany or England. Census records indicate that he was born in Germany in October, 1876 and his father was English and his mother was German. There are other sources that state that he was born in Cincinnati, Ohio. He married Henrietta C. Sommer sometime in 1898. Henrietta was born in New Jersey in February, 1874 and her mother and father were German. Charles Clifton Howard, their son, was born in Jersey City, New Jersey on July 19, 1899. The 1900 census for New Jersey indicates that they lived in Union City, Hudson County, New Jersey and his occupation was that of a bookkeeper.

Charles Clifton Howard was the father of Terris Clifton Howard, William Duncan Howard; grandfather of Terry Charles Howard, Doreen Annette Howard, Jeanette Aileen Howard and Duncan Christopher Howard.

Sometime around 1908, William Howard changed his name to William August Howell for the American stage and married Myra Velma Smith. They lived in Monticello, Sullivan County, New York where their daughter, Constance Jeannette Howell, was born and in Bronx, New York City where William Augustus Howell was born. The family moved to Los Angeles, California prior to the 1920 census for California. William Augustus Howell was Kathleen Howell's father.

William August Howell also used the name Anders Van Haden during his Hollywood career along with the name of William Anders Howell during his radio appearances. Besides his acting career, he wrote numerous radio scripts and was an accomplished watercolor painter.

Family History

Four Generations

This photograph may have been taken about 1904 when Maria Wilhelmj possibly performed at the World's Fair in St. Louis, Missouri.

Back Row: Unidentified, Henrietta C. Sommer, wife of William A. Howard; William A. Howard, Front Row: Maria Gastell Wilhelmj, Charles C. Howard, Unidentified, Unidentified. (Photo from collection of Terris C. Howard).

Anders Van Haden

Of German origin, William Van Haden began his stage career around 1895 appearing in German-language plays under the name of William A. Howell (or, as he was sometimes billed, W.A. Howell). After touring with several also-ran stock companies, Van Haden entered films with the Kalem company in 1911, appearing opposite that company's first leading lady, Gene Gauntier. He later worked for Rex, Biograph, and Thanhouser, starring in and directing a series of Falstaff comedies for the latter. Lensed in Florida, the Falstaff films were polite little situation comedies featuring Howell/Van Haden as a dapper gent with a thin mustache and looking for all the world like the later Charley Chase. He left Thanhouser to operate his own company, the short-lived Gotham Film Co., which produced "patriotic spectacles." By the 1920s, he was playing bit parts in low-budget Westerns but apparently did direct the still extant Jesus of Nazareth (1928), a screen pageant featuring Philip Van Loan as Christ and Anna Lehr (mother of actress Ann Dvorak) as the Virgin Mary. After the advent of sound, Van Haden became a busy performer in German-language versions of such Grade-A Hollywood productions as The Trial of Mary Dugan (1930) and The Big Trail (1931) but was offered mainly bit parts in more mainstream English-language fare.

Hans J. Wollstein, Movie Critic
(Permission to use granted by Hans J. Wollstein)

William A. Howell. Myra had written Stage, New York City.
(Photo from the collection of Myra Van Haden)

Anders Van Haden

Anders Van Haden
October, 1876 - June 19, 1936
(Photo from the collection of Myra Van Haden)

ANDERS VAN HADEN, MOVIE MAN IS DEAD

HOLLYWOOD (UP) — Anders Van Haden, pioneer motion picture actor, director, writer and producer, died yesterday from an attack of heart disease. He was 59 years old.

Van Haden entered pictures in 1910 and was connected with the industry until a few years ago.

He was born in Cleveland, O., in 1877 and went on the stage in 1895. Besides his widow, he is survived by two children.

The Star Journal, Sandusky, Ohio,
Saturday, June 20, 1936.
(Permission to use granted by the Sandusky Register).

Veteran Producer Dies

HOLLYWOOD, June 20 (UP).— Anders Van Haden, pioneer motion picture actor, director, writer and producer, died yesterday of an attack of heart disease. He was 59 years old. Van Haden entered pictures in 1910.

Charleston Daily Mail,
Sunday, June 21, 1936.

FINAL CURTAIN

Billboard reported that Anders Van Haden died in the Hollywood Hospital on June 19, 1936. Also in the article that he entered the movie industry in 1910 and was later associated with Thanhouser], Rex, Biograph and Gotham productions.

Anders Van Haden

DEATHS

The death of Anders Van Haden was reported by The Los Angeles Times on June 19, 1936. The article mentioned his wife Myra Van Haden, Constance Herrmann, William A. Howell and Charles C. Howard.

Anders Van Haden, Film Pioneer, Dies

Anders Van Haden, producer, director, actor and writer of early motion picture days, yesterday followed the old master of the silent films, Henry B. Walthall, into death. He was 59.

Victim of a heart attack, Mr. Van Haden died at the Hollywood Hospital, leaving a widow and two children. He was once a power in such companies as Tannhauser, Rex, Biograph and Gotham.

Los Angeles Examiner, Sunday, June 20, 1936.

OBITUARIES

ANDERS VAN HADEN

The obituary of Anders Van Haden was reported by Variety on June 14, 1936. The obituary mentioned that he was an actor and director in silent films and a bit character actor in late years. It also mentioned that his widow and three children survive.

DEATHS

With Funeral Announcements

VAN HADEN-June 19. Anders Van Haden, beloved husband of Myra Vilma Van Haden, loving father of Constance Herrmann, William A. Howell and Charles C. Howard. Services, 3 p.m., Monday, at Pierce Brothers.

Los Angeles Evening Herald-Express, Saturday Morning, June 19, 1936.

Film Pioneer's Service Planned

Funeral services today were arranged for Monday at 3 p. m. for Anders Van Haden, 59, pioneer motion picture actor, director, writer and producer, who died yesterday from an attack of heart disease. The funeral will be held in the Pierce Brothers Chapel.

Like H. B. Walthall, his friend, Mr. Van Haden entered pictures in 1910 and was connected with the industry until a few years ago.

His death came on the day last rites were being quietly conducted for Mr. Walthall in Beverly Hills.

During the early days of the industry, Mr. Van Haden was affiliated with such companies as Tannhauser [Thanhouser], Rex, Biograph and Gotham.

He was born in Cleveland, O., and went on the stage in 1895. Besides his widow, he is survived by two children.

Hollywood Citizen-News, Saturday, June 20, 1936.

STAGE

The attempt here is to list all known stage performances by William A. Howell (AKA Anders Van Haden). Information for the majority of these listings came from the 1908 diary of William A. Howell, which notes some theatrical schedules and performances. The diary really yielded much more information after writing many libraries throughout the United States about the possible names of plays, roles, etc. that were listed. Responses from the libraries or historical societies have provided the newspaper clippings presented here. Other information was gleaned from known performance schedules and various newspaper articles or other publications. This list is not complete by any means and is presented to give an impression of his stage career.

It was reported by the Syracuse Herald in May 1936, that Anders Van Haden made his debut with Daly's Stock Company in 1890 under the direction of Augustin Daly. William A. Howell was an actor and a director for Poli's New England Theatres. He also acted in the German theatre in New York and Philadelphia. He was in the Gage Stock Company under the direction of Frederick 'Fred' Gage, *Her Mad Marriage* under the direction of H. W. Rosenthal, the Adam Stock Company under the direction of Monte Thompson, the Graustark Dramatic Company under the direction of A. G. Delamater and the Louis James Touring Company under the direction of Louis James. He also thought to have worked for the Kyrle Bellew's Company.

William A. Howell
(Photo from collection of
Myra Van Haden).

William A. Howell
(Photo from collection of
Myra Van Haden).

7

Gage Stock Company

Tour Schedule -1907

Aug	26	New Bedford, Mass.
Sep	2	- do
	9	Fall River,"
	16	Biddeford, Me.
	23	Bangor,"
	30	Augusta,"
Oct	7	Waterville,"
	14	Rockland,"
	28	Berlin, N.H.
Nov	4	Portsmouth,"
	11	Lawrence, Mass.
	18	Haverhill,"
	25	Salem,"
Dec	2	Lowell,"
	9	Lynn,"
	16	Portland, Me.
	23	Lewiston,"

From the 1908 Diary of William A. Howell.

CORRESPONDENCE.
MASSACHUSETTS.

FALL RIVER.— SAVOY (Julius Cahn, lessee and mgr.: William D. Reed, res. mgr.): Gage Stock co. 9-14 (daily matinees) opened their engagement 9, presenting At Old Point Comfort (matinee) and Her Sweetest Sin (night); the co. is headed by Will. A. Howell and Rita Davis, both of whom were very good; the productions are well staged and the supporting co. up to the average. Other plays: Hearts Adrift, The Little Minister, Her Terrible Secret, Sapho, and The Parish Priest; attendance first half of week good.

The New York Dramatic Mirror,
Saturday, September 21, 1907.

The Portsmouth Daily Herald on Tuesday, November 5, 1907 reported that the Gage Stock Company opened its engagement at Music Hall on Monday evening, presenting as the first attraction "The Parish Priest."

The part of Father Whalen was played by Walter Befell, Dr. Edward Gage was played by Frederick Gage, James Gage was played by William A. Howell and Rita Davis was worthy of as Nellie Durkin.

Gage company, which is booked at the Academy of Music for this whole week, as reported Haverhill Evening Gazette on November 19, 1907 opened their engagement yesterday with a presentation of "Land of Cotton."

The cast composed of Mr. William A. Howell and Miss Rita Davis in the lead. Miss Halved proves herself and Mr. Fairfax is also a capable in his ways.

The Salem Evening News on November 26, 1907 reported that the Gage Stock Company presented the "Parish Priest" to a large audience at the Empire Theatre last night. The cast of characters was as follows: The cast of characters was Walter Befell as Rev. Father Whalen, Frederick Gage as Dr. Edward Welch, William A. Howell as James Welch, Bernard Fairfax as Dr. Cassidy, Rita Davis as Nellie Durkin and other capable actors.

The Lowell Courier-Citizen on Tuesday, December 3, 1907 reported that "The Parish Priest" played at the Opera House last evening to a good audience.

Father Whalen was played by Walter Befell, Dr. Edward Welch was played by Frederick Gage, Nellie Durkin the sweet heroine played by Rita Davis, Katherine Corrigan was played by Miss M. Halle, Agnes Cassidy was played by Miss R. Vernon. James Welch was played by William A. Howell, Michael Sullivan was played by Milford and Dr. Cassidy was played by Bernard Fairfax.

Her Mad Marriage

Tour Schedule - 1908

Feb 1 Started Rehearsal
      3 Taunton, [Mass] rehrd-
      4   rehrd
      5   rehrd
      6   rehrd
      7   rehrd
      8 Left by boat for Fall
          River, then to Lowell
   10 Lowell [Mass]
   11   do
   12   do
   13 Worcester [Mass]
          Signed with J. Thompson
          (written in diary)
   14 Fitchburg [Mass]
          layd off at Worcester
          (written in diary)
   15 Haverhill [Mass]
   17 Gloucester [Mass]
   18 Lawrence [Mass]
   19   do
   20 Fall River [Mass]
   21   do
   22   do
   23 Back to Fall River
          and boat to New York
   24 New Bedford [Mass]
          Cancelled, NYDM,
          February 29, 1908.
   25 Taunton [Mass]
   26 Attleboro [Mass]
   27 Woonsocket [RI]
   28 Brockton [Mass]
   29 do

From the 1908 Diary of William A. Howell.

OPERA HOUSE

❖

"HER MAD MARRIAGE."

Jean Barrymore's thrilling four-act detective romance, "Her Mad Marriage," was played at the Opera House last night, and an audience which was thoroughly appreciative witnessed the performance. The title is an excellent index of the story of the play, and as may be inferred the four acts are crowded with thrills.

The leading character is a detective, Bruce Benton, who has the faculty of being Johnny-on-the-spot when his services are required. Bruce Benton was a good detective, and he foiled many of the villainous schemes of the villainous villain. The role was ably essayed by Orrin T. Burke. William D. Howell as Noel Norman, alias Black Donald, was the bad man, and he certainly was all that a melodrama villain should be. Nothing was beyond Noel Norman, not even the hurling of deadly bombs, the cracking of a safe or an abduction. All of these sets were engineered by Norman, and that they were not all carried out was due solely to the sleuthing of Bruce Benton.

The remainder of the company included Lon H. Burton as Toothless Dike, Noel Norman's assistant; Harry L. Baker, Frank M. Lolan, J. Paul Jones, Amy Shaffer Barrymore, Celia Rosewood and Marie Barker, all of whom did their share in making the production enjoyable. 'Her Mad Marriage" will be repeated tonight and tomorrow afternoon and night.

Unidentified newspaper article, 1908.
(From the collection of Mya Van Haden).

Her Mad Marriage

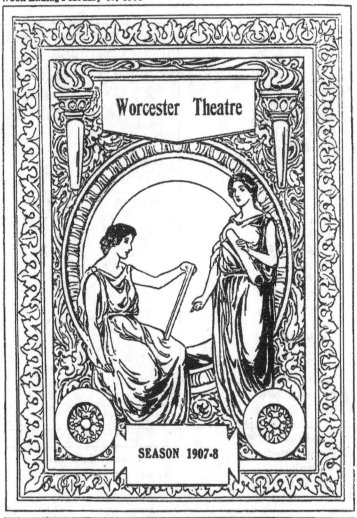

Program of Her Mad Marriage.
(Program from collection of Myra Van Haden).

Her Mad Marriage

Worcester Theatre Program   11

VALENTINES

St. Valentine's Day-Is not forgotten or passed lightly by--It has been observed for over 560 years. We have an especially select showing of artistic novelties at very attractive prices. Main Floor.

ONE DAY, THURSDAY, MATINE AND NIGHT,

THE ROSENTHAL AMUSEMENT CO. (INC.)

Presents the Thrilling Detective Romance,

HER MAD MARRIAGE

BY JEAN BARRYMORE

CAST OF CHARACTERS.

Bruce Benton, a young detective......................Orrin T. Burke
Noel Norman, alias Black Donald......................Wm. D. Howell
Toothles Dike, Norman's tool.........................Lon H. Burton
Judge Thornton, a banker.............................Harry L. Barker
Tatters, a genuine hobo..............................J. Paul Jones
Malone, Officer No. 23...............................Frank M. Dolan
Nadga Thornton, known as the Queen.............Amy Shaffer Barrymore
Mabel Thornton, the abducted child.................Celia Rosewood
Ginger, a lady of color..............................Marie Barker

11

Her Mad Marriage

The "Bon Contour" Bust Supporter. Miss Lyons, 270 Main St.

FOR THE ROSENTHAL AMUSEMENT CO. (INC.)

H. W. Rosenthal	General Manager
Wm. D. Howell,	Stage Manager
Irving Lesser	Business Manager
Al. J. Roscoe	Carpenter
Frank Dennison	Representative

MUSICAL PROGRAM

The Orchestra, under the direction of Mr. D. Silvéster, will render the following selections:

MARCH—"Yankee Grit"	Holzman
OVERTURE—"Bonnie Scotland"	Catlin
SONG—"Kentucky Babe"	Geibel
MEXICAN IDYL—"On the Mesa-Grande"	Maurice
CHARACTERISTIC—"Every Little Bit Added"	Dillon
SELECTION—"The Sho-Gun"	Luders

French Flannel Dressing Sacques. Miss Lyons, 270 Main St.

Peruchi - Gypzene Stock Company

The stock company of Peruchi-Gypzene had at least three different tour locations - Columbia, South Carolina; Knoxville, Tennessee and Macon, Georgia with Chelso D. Peruchi, manager.

Tour Schedule - 1908

May 1 Start 12:30 PM
          for Columbia, S.C.
      3 Arrive Columbia City
          Hotel, S.C.
      7 start rehearsal
          Man's Enemy
    11 Man's Enemy, Harry
    14 Charity Ball, John
    18 New Dominion, Baron
    21 Way Down East, Allen
    25 The Idlev, Mark Cross
    28 Little Alabama, Col. Groves
Jun 1 Confusion, Mortimer
      4 Man Outside, Gilbert Elton
      7 Macon, Ga, Crump's Pk
      8 Charity Ball
    11 Cloverdale, Frank Harlow
    15 Man From Mexico
          Warden [Lovell]
    18 Alabama, Col. Groves
    22 New Dominion, Baron
    25 Confusion, Mortimer
    29 Tribly, Taffy
Jul 2 Ensign B.B.
      4 Ensign, Confusion
      6 Slaves of Russia, Ivan
      9 Lost Paradise, Ruben
    19 left for Savannah [Ga]
    20 Savannah, left for
          Phila[delphia]
    21 On sea
    22 do
    23 Arrive Phila[delphia]
          left for NY
    24 N.Y.
    25 left for Boston

From the 1908 Diary of William A. Howell.

HYATT PARK CASINO.

Mr. and Mrs. Chelso D. Peruchi arrived in the city yesterday from Jacksonville and will remain here for about three weeks, giving his personal supervision to the arrangements for opening Hyatt Park casino for the summer. all the members of the company have also arrived and the first rehearsal of the season will be held this afternoon. Also there are 15 members of the company in the city and Mr. Peruchi says that the people of Columbia will have reason to congratulate themselves on securing such a strong cast. He has very carefully selected the company which is to play at the Hyatt Park casino and all are experienced and capable.

The casino has been remodeled and will seat about 400 more than last season. The seats are now on an inclined floor and every seat in the house is a "good one." The casino will also be cooler this season, as it has been mad more open. The natural ventilation is not only improved, but when the weather begins to get warmer additional electric fans will be installed. No pains will be spared to make the casino comfortable and Mr. Peruchi says that the cast of the company will be such as to appeal to the Columbia summer theatregoers.

Peruchi - Gypzene Stock Company

The casino will open on next Monday night with "The Sergeant of the Guard," a beautiful society comedy-drama which is bound to appeal to all classes, besides giving the new company a swell opportunity to show their ability. Mr. Peruchi and Miss Gypzene, who proved exceedingly popular last season, will appear in roaring comedy roles. Miss Caroline Klohr, the only other member of the company who was seen here last season, and who won the hearts of all, will appear in the role of the leading lady.

The other members of the company are as follows: William C. Howell, leading man; Herbert C. Pardy, character actor; Earle P. Adams, stage director and comedian; Sidney Platt, juvenile; William Raymond, light comedian; George Foulk, heavy, George C. Wood, genteel heavy; Harry Dickeson, business manager; Miss Georgia Francis, character actress; Miss Raymond, ingénue; Miss Willie Brown, soubrette.

The sale of seats is now on at Thomas' drug store. The Ladies' Juvenile orchestra will dispense music 15 minutes before each performance. The curtain will go up at 8:30 on the opening night.

The State, Columbia, S.C., Thursday Morning, May 7, 1908.
(Permission to use granted by islandpacket.com)

HYATT PARK CASINO.

Tomorrow night will witness the opening of Hyatt Park casino for the summer season, with the popular Peruchi-Gypzene company playing "The Sergeant of the Guard," a society comedy-drama that is sure to be well received. The casino has been remodeled and will seat about 400 more persons than last season, with every seat in the theatre a good one, furnishing a plain view of the stage at all times. New chairs and stage furniture and scenery have been installed and Mr. Peruchi announces that further improvements will be made during the season.

The street railway company will put on an extra complement of cars tomorrow evening to handle the crowds. The curtain will go up promptly at 8:30 and there will be two hours filled with rollicking comedy. This season's cast includes 15 members, all of whom have had several years' experience on the stage. The cast for "The Sergeant of the Guard" has been carefully selected and all handle their parts well, as demonstrated at yesterday's rehearsal. The ladies' juvenile orchestra will dispense music for 15 minutes before each performance and some clever inter-act specialties are down on the programme.

It is expected that the casino will be well filled the opening night, but Mr. Peruchi announces that he hopes to have seats for all who come out. This company "made good" last season and the fact that Mr. Peruchi is bringing a larger and higher salaried company here for this season entitles the Hyatt Park casino to a generous patronage.

Peruchi - Gypzene Stock Company

The members of the Peruchi-Gypzene company already on hand are: Chelso D. Peruchi and Miss Mabel Gypzene, who need no word of commendation; William C. Howell, leading man, late of the Kyrle-Bellews company; Earle P. Adams, stage director and comedian, formerly principal comedian in his stock company in Boston and late stage director of the Pittsburgh opera house; Herbert C. Pardy, character actor, late of the Grand Opera House Stock company in Philadelphia and Klaw & Erlanger attractions; William Raymond, light comedian, and George Foulk, heavy, formerly of high class New York companies, including Miss Anglin's; Miss Caroline Klohr, leading lady, well known and popular in Columbia; Miss Georgia Francis, character actress, formerly of the Grand opera house stock in Philadelphia and Klaw & Erlanger attractions; Miss Raymond, ingénue, late of the "Lion and the Mouse" company; Miss Winnie Brown, soubrette, formerly with the Shubert companies.

Mr. Harry Dickeson, the business manager for Mr. Peruchi in Columbia, came her direct from New York. He is a man of wide experience in the theatrical business and has been acquainted with Mr. Peruchi for a number of years.

Miss Mabel Paige, who has appeared before Columbia audiences on numerous occasions, will be seen here two weeks out of each two months. she is playing the role of the leading lady at Mr. Peruchi's Jacksonville theatre, the Phoenix Park casino at present.

The prices of admission will be the same as last season. Tickets are on sale at Thomas' drug store, where they may be purchased at any time before 6 o'clock each afternoon.

The State, Columbia, S.C., Sunday Morning, May 10, 1908.
(Permission to use granted by islandpacket.com)

HYATT PARK CASINO.

A large and representative audience witnessed the presentation of "A Mid-night Marriage" at Hyatt Park casino last evening. It is a very catchy comedy-drama and gave the company an opportunity to display their real merit. The play "caught on" instantly and proved a decidedly popular attraction.

Messrs. Howell and Platt, as two brothers-one a preacher and the other a gambler-were unusually good and made a hit. Mr. Peruchi played Judge Knox, and did so in his own inimitable style, and Miss Gypzene was clever and captivating as Bess. Earle P. Adams, as Alex, was usually good.

Clever specialties were introduced by Mr. Peruchi, Miss Gypzene, Earle P. Adams, Miss Brown and Mr. Foulk.

The same play will be presented again this evening and tomorrow afternoon and evening. The matinee for ladies and children tomorrow should be well patronized.

Terris C. Howard

Peruchi - Gypzene Stock Company

Mr. Peruchi is more than pleased with the generous patronage given the casino thus early in the season and the gradual increase shown in the sizes of the audiences indicates that this will be the most successful season in the history of Hyatt Park amusement houses.

The State, Columbia, S.C., Friday Morning, May 15, 1908.
(Permission to use granted by islandpacket.com)

HYATT PARK CASINO.

"A Midnight Marriage," the beautiful domestic comedy-drama, which is now playing at the Hyatt Park casino, is a very catchy production and is being well received. A good sized audience was present last night, but the real large crowd of the season is expected at this afternoon's matinee, the first matinee of the season.

The cast of characters in this play is as follows:

John Van Buren, W. A. Howell; Dick Van Buren, Sidney Platt; Alexander Robinson, Earl P. Adams; Paxton, Archie Foulk; Crayton, Arthur Evans; Cruger, Herbert Pardey; Betts, Frank Raymond; Judge Knox, Chelso D. Peruchi; Ann Kruger, Miss Caroline Klohr; Mrs. Van Buren, Miss Clara Baxter; Sofia, Miss Jessie Brown; Phyllis Lee, Miss Leonie Raymond; Mrs. DePyster, Miss Georgia Francis; Bessie, Miss Mabel Gypzene; Cain, Master Raymond.

It is the largest as well as decidedly the strongest cast yet seen in a production at this popular summer theatre. Mr. Howell, leading man, is a strong character actor and shows that he has had long experience on the stage. Sidney Platt, who takes the part of one of the Van Buren brothers, is also good. Earl P. Adams and Miss Mabel Gypzene, in their comedy roles, are very clever and received generous applause. Mr. Peruchi, as Judge Knox, has a part to which he is especially adapted. It offers opportunity for high class humor of the rollicking kind, and to use a slang expression, he "is there with the goods." Miss Georgia Francis is also extremely clever and accomplished in the role of Mrs. DePyster and the sketches furnished by her and Mr. Peruchi called forth loud applause. Miss Leonie Raymond had one of the strongest parts and handled it with ease. Miss Caroline Klohr, always popular with the Columbia audiences, was good as Miss Ann Kruger.

Mr. Peruchi has good singers with his company this year and the between-act specialties last night are unusually pleasing. Mr. Earl P. Adams made a big hit last night with his negro dialect songs. The other specialties last night were by Mr. Foulk and Miss Brown, both very clever singers.

Matinee this afternoon and final performance of "A Midnight Marriage" tonight.

The State, Columbia, S.C., Saturday Morning, May 16, 1908.
(Permission to use granted by islandpacket.com)

Peruchi - Gypzene Stock Company

HYATT PARK CASINO.

The first matinee of the season at Hyatt Park casino was well patronized yesterday and the audience of ladies and children was extremely generous in their applause-and the play was worth it all. Mr. Peruchi's comedy work in this performance was well worth the price of admission. The specialties are superior to those seen at this playhouse last season and attracted much favorable comment.

Another large audience greeted the company again last night, and gradually the patronage is increasing. Mr. Peruchi states that the company now playing at Hyatt Park is one of the strongest ever seen at a summer theatre in the South.

Monday night "Hearts and Flowers," a down-East comedy-drama will be presented, with Mr. William Howell as leading man. Mr. Howell has starred in this performance for the past several years and his work is bound to please all who witness the presentation of this popular play the first three nights of this week. Miss Klohr will appear in the role of the leading lady.

There will be a change of programme Thursday night, "Man's Inhumanity" being put on the boards. This latter production will be presented for three nights and Saturday afternoon.

The between-act specialties will be clever. Mr. Pat Crawford, a well known Columbia minstrel man, has been engaged and will appear each night during the week in black-face comedy and dancing specialties. He has worked with one of the leading minstrel shows the past year and shows decided improvement over his work of last season.

Reserved seats may be secured at Thomas' drug store.

The State, Columbia, S.C., Sunday Morning, May 17, 1908.
(Permission to use granted by islandpacket.com)

HYATT PARK CASINO.

Despite the threatening weather last night a good-sized audience witnessed the initial performance of "Hearts and Flowers," the pretty absorbing play picturing life in the hills of Virginia. the play is laid just after the close of the Civil war and deals with life among the aristocrats of the grand Old Dominion State. It is one of the prettiest plays ever staged at Hyatt Park casino.

Mr. Wm. A. Howell, who plays the leading part, made a distinct hit last night. He has starred in this production for a number of years and his interpretation of Baron Franz Victor von Hohenstauffen is par excellence. The full cast is as follows:

Baron Franz Victor von Hohenstauffen, Wm. A. Howell; Edgar Norman Randolph, Herbert Pardey; Marshall Boner, Archie Foulk; Charles McVeigh, Sidney Platt; Uncle Poly, George Raymond; Martha (a poor relation), Miss Jessie Brown; Mrs. Randolph (Flora's stepmother), Miss Georgia Francis; Mrs. Josephine Dulaney, Miss Leonie Raymond; Flora May Randolph, Miss Caroline Klohr.

Peruchi - Gypzene Stock Company

Pat Crawford, the well known Columbia comedian, was greeted with loud applause. His between-act specialties are good and he is one of the cleverest "funny men" seen here for some time. He deserves to have a large house every night this week, not solely because he is a Columbia boy, but because his work is clever and well worth seeing.

"Hearts and Flowers" again tonight and tomorrow night. Advance sale of reserved seat tickets at Thomas' drug store.

The State, Columbia, S.C., Tuesday Morning, May 19, 1908.
(Permission to use granted by islandpacket.com)

HYATT PARK CASINO.

"Man's Inhumanity," the pretty pastoral drama, depicting country life in the East, is one of the strongest plays yet presented the Peruchi-Gypzene company in this city and deserves a good house this afternoon and tonight.

A story of a beautiful girl wronged by a demon in the garb of a gentleman-her life made miserable by him on every hand. She goes far from home, away out into the country, and strives to forget her past and begin life anew. By a strange coincidence the designing scoundrel who had turned her promise of a life of sunshine into the sad reality of darkness and despair becomes a visitor at this same country home, where Ruth Walton has gone, in search of a ray of hope and a speck of friendly fellowship.

The forlorn and disconsolate girl gets a warm welcome after some misgivings natural with these good, honest country folk of New England, and the past is rapidly fading from her memory and she is beginning to get back her rosy cheeks and vivaciousness when Dwight Bradley, the man of all men whom she would not see, appears on the scene. His coming supplants sunshine with sadness and lest Ruth interfere with his plans he schemes to get her out of the way. His money is scorned; his threats to the girl are in vain, but a mere whisper about the girl's past life starts the gossips in the neighborhood and this all but loses for Ruth her new-made friends and the home which she had won.

But - the sturdy New England sentiment is not so easily affected. The truth is learned, gradually, and Ruth retains her home, her friends, and Dwight Bradley is brought to a full realization of his shame, and, scoffed and scorned, he is kicked out to suffer the jeers of a righteous community and the pangs of an awakened conscience.

Miss Klohr, in the role of Ruth Walton, displays strong dramatic ability and her interpretation of this difficult character part is unusually good. Miss Raymond is equally clever as Mabel Halstead, a part which demands strong acting with occasional touches of comedy. Mr. Howell plays the part of Allen Shaw, the lover and defender of Ruth Walton; George Raymond takes the part of Martin Shaw, the old farmer; Archie Foulk plays the heavy; Herbert Pardy as Timothy Dawson, the eccentric and forgetful professor; Miss Francis, as the comical old maid, and Mr. Earle P. Adams appears as Si Hawkins, the man of all work.

18

Peruchi - Gypzene Stock Company

The play is enlivened by the clever comedy work of Mr. Adams, who is decidedly one of the cleverest as well as most versatile comedians seen in this city.

The same play will be presented again this afternoon and tonight. The ladies' matinee is at 3:30; the evening performance at 8:30 p. m. sharp. Tickets on sale at Thomas' drug store.

The State, Columbia, S.C., Saturday Morning, May 23, 1908.
(Permission to use granted by islandpacket.com)

HYATT PARK CASINO.

"The Fatal Rose of Red," a beautiful psychological drama, was presented by the Peruchi-Gypzene company last night at the Hyatt Park casino. It was so well played by the company that it would be hard to individualize. the play itself is such a high class order that death-like stillness prevailed during the dramatic scenes and the high class comedy interspersed was happily placed.

The much heralded "Billy" Beard came for his share of applause as he made his appearance after the second act. It was plainly seen that he is the same popular Billy Beard humorous, magnetic and a hit. His jokes and songs were all new and he can be proud of the reception of his work. The house was well filled and if Manager Peruchi had heard the public comment as the audience left the theatre, both he and his stage director, Earl P. Adams, might have felt just pride.

"The Fatal rose of Red" will be played until Wednesday night making room for "Little Alabama" Thursday and the rest of the week. Following is the cast of characters in the play no on the boards:

Mark Cross, Will A. Howell; Sir John Harding, Archie Foulk; Simeon Strong, from America, Earl P. Adams; Gen. Merriweather, Herbert Pardey; Bennett, Cross' man, George Raymond; Mrs. Cross, Miss Georgia Francis; Kate Merriweather, Helen's stepsister, Miss Jessie Brown; Lady Harding, Miss Caroline Klohr.

The State, Columbia, S.C., Tuesday Morning, May 26, 1908.
(Permission to use granted by islandpacket.com)

HYATT PARK CASINO.

Another large audience greeted "The Fatal Rose of Red: at the Hyatt Park casino last night. This is one of the strongest dramatic productions ever seen at the park, and will be presented for the last time this evening. Clean, wholesome comedy is appropriately interspersed and the play is one which pleases. Mr. Howell and Miss Klohr play the leading parts.

Billy Beard was greeted with rounds of applause last night. This Columbia comedian is very popular with the patrons of the casino and received frequent encores last night. He will appear each night during the week and at the special bargain matinee Saturday afternoon.

Terris C. Howard

Peruchi - Gypzene Stock Company

"Little Alabama" will be presented the last three nights in the week.

Reserved seats are on sale at Thomas' drug store.

The State, Columbia, S.C., Wednesday Morning, May 27, 1908.
(Permission to use granted by islandpacket.com)

HYATT PARK CASINO.

The Southern romance of ante-bellum days, "Little Alabama," will be presented tonight and for the remainder of the week at Hyatt Park casino. The crowds at the park have been gradually increasing and the indications are that the Peruchi-Gypzene company will have a most successful season.

Mr. and Mrs. Peruchi will return Sunday from their Knoxville theatre and will be seen all week, beginning Monday, June 1, in a beautiful comedy.

"Billy" Beard appears between acts all the week, including the special matinee Saturday afternoon.

The following is the cast of the play for tonight and the remainder of the week in "Little Alabama."

Col. Grove, a slave holder, Will A. Howell; Caspar, a slave, Archie Foulk; Robert Perrin, a young planter, Herbert Pardy; Pete, a colored boy, Arthur Evans; Johnson, "jes plain neggah," George Raymond; Mandy, his wife, Earle P. Adams; Little Alabama, Miss Jessie Brown; Leota Grove, Miss Raymond; Sue, wife of Caspar, Georgia Francis; Mrs.

Mary Grove, the colonel's wife, Miss Caroline Klohr.

The State, Columbia, S.C., Thursday Morning, May 28, 1908.
(Permission to use granted by islandpacket.com)

HYATT PARK CASINO.

The audience at Hyatt Park casino was considerably larger last night than for several evenings previous and "Little Alabama" made a great hit. The play is based upon a Southern romance of ante-bellum days and is "catchy" and absorbing, a play that is sure to please.

Cast of characters: Col. Grove, a slave holder, Will A. Howell; Caspar, a slave, Archie Foulk; Robert Perrin, a young planter, Herbert Pardy; Pete, a colored boy, Arthur Evans; Johnson, "jes plain niggah," George Raymond' Mandy, his wife, Earle P. Adams; Little Alabama, Miss Jessie Brown; Leota Grove, Miss Raymond; Sue, wife of Caspar, Georgia Francis; Mrs. Mary Grove, the colonel's wife, Miss Caroline Klohr.

"Billy" Beard was greeted with loud applause last night. He has a bunch of brand new jokes and jokelets that will make a dispeptic [dyspeptic] laugh until his sides ache.

The State, Columbia, S.C., Friday Morning, May 29, 1908.
(Permission to use granted by islandpacket.com)

Peruchi - Gypzene Stock Company

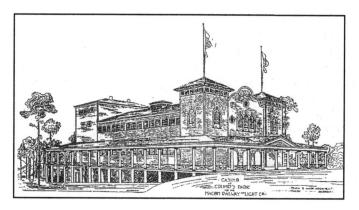

Crumps Park Casino, Macon, Georgia. The Macon Daily Telegraph, May 21, 1905.
(Courtesy of the Middle Georgia Archives, Washington Memorial Library).

The Macon Daily Telegraph on June 9, 1908 reported that the play "A Midnight Marriage" by the Peruchi-Gypzene Company was well received by the audience at the Casino. The cast consisted of William A. Howell, the leading man as the Rev. John Van Buren, Misses Leola Raymond, Carolina Klohr, and Mr. Sidney Platt.

As reported by the Macon Daily Telegraph on June 16, 1908, the play "The Man from Mexico" by the Peruchi-Gypzene Company was proven to the complete satisfaction of the Macon theater-going audience at the Casino.

The cast of characters were Mr. Archie Polk as Sheriff Cook, Mr. Peruchi as Benjamin Fitzhew, Miss Gypzene as Mrs. Benjamin Fitzhew, Sidney Platt as Edward Farrier, Edward Raymond as Richard Danton, Earl P. Adams as Mr. Majors, William Howell as Warden Lovell and other wonderful actors.

The Macon Daily Telegraph on June 19, 1908 reported the play of "Little Alabama" at Crump's Park Casino by the Peruchi-Gypzene Company was the most interesting melodrama ever shown here.

The parts of the cast were well acted by William A. Howell as Col. Preston Grove, Archie Foulk as Casper, Miss Caroline Klohr as Mrs. Grove, Sydney Platt as Pete, Miss Lela Raymond as Leola Grove, Earl P. Adams as Many, Miss Jessie Brown as Little Alabama George Raymond as Johnson Herbert Paedy as Robert Perrin and Miss Georgia Francis as Sue.

The Macon Daily Telegraph on June 26, 1908 reported on the play "Trilby" by the Peruchi-Gypzene Company at Crump's Park Casino. A difficult play requiring actors to fit the roles of which they had no trouble with.

Miss Caroline Klohr played the title role, Mr. Will. J. Irvine played the role of Svengali, Mr. William A.

Howell played the role of Taffy, Mr. Earl P. Adams played the role of Little Billie.

The play "The Naval Hero" by the Peruchi-Gypzene Company at Crump's Park Casino was reported by The Macon Daily Telegraph on July 3, 1908. The play was the most enjoyable performance and received well by the audience

Mr. William A. Howell was the leading actor, Miss Klohr in leading feminine role. Also appearing were Mr. Will A. Irwin, Miss Raymond, Me. Earle P. Way.

Adam Good Stock Company

Tour Schedule - 1908

Sep	21	New London [Conn]
	28	Woonsocket [RI]
Oct	5	Fitchsburg [Mass]
	12	Fall River [Mass]
	19	New Bedford [Mass]
	26	Newport, RI
Nov	2	Brockton [Mass]
	5	Closed
		(written in diary)
	9	Marlborough, Mass
	16	Portland, Ma[ine]
	23	Bangor,"
	30	Lewiston,"
Dec	4	Lawrence, Mass
	14	Lowell,"
	21	Haverhill [Mass]
	28	Salem [Mass]
		Pittsfield [Mass]

*From the 1908
Diary of William A. Howell.*

CORRESPONDENCE. MASSACHUSETTS.

FALL RIVER. -ACADEMY (Julius Cahn, lessee and mgr.: George S. Wiley, res. mgr.): Adam Good co. 12-17 opened their engagement 12, presenting Lena Rivers; The Undertow was the bill 13; The Little Gray Lady (matinee) and A Texas Ranger (night) was presented 14; the co. is headed by Helen Pongee, and includes Sadie Gal loupe, Will A. Howell, Mabel Ward and J. Warren Chase; pleased good attendance.

w. f. gee.

The Newport Daily News reported on October 27, 1908 that the Adam Good Stock Company opened at the Opera House last night and presented "The Little Gray Lady" to a large audience. Helen Pingree had the title role of the heroine, William A. Howell enacted the leading male role, Sadie Calliope, as the man catcher, Georgia Phil as the boarding house keeper and H. Blosser Jennings as her husband, J. F. Monsey as Richard Graham, Katherine Francis as his secret bride, J. Warren Chase as the secret service man, and James L. Dempsey as the ubiquitous boy.

Cast pose with transportation, William Howell, far right.
(Photo from collection of Myra Van Haden)

Graustark

The dramatic company of Graustark had three different tours-Central, Eastern and Western. William A. Howell was with the Central Graustark dramatic Company, A. G. Delamater, manager. The diary of William Howell indicated rehearsal and a tour schedule of Graustark. I have included a schedule derived from The New York Dramatic Mirror that indicates a few differences in the dates but also takes the schedule up through May 15, 1909.

The biggest difference in the two schedules was the December 7th to 12th engagement at the Yorkville Theatre, New York City.

Tour Schedule - 1908/1909

Nov	13	Rehearsed Graustark
	16	Rehearsed Graustark
	17	do
	18	do
	25	Booton, NJ
	26	Middletown, NY
	27	Peekskill [NY]
	28	Kingston [NY]
	29	do
	30	Catskill [NY]
Dec	1	Poughkeepsie [NY]
	2	Schenectady [NY]
	3	Glens Falls [NY]
	4	Hoosick Falls [NY]
	5	N. Adams, Mass
	7	Granville, NY
	8	Rutland, VT
	9	Burlington, VT
	10	Barre, VT
	11	Randolph, VT
	12	Claremont, NH
	14	Bellows Falls, VT
	15	Keene, NH
	16	Newport, NH
	17	St. Johnsbury [VT]
	18	St. Albans [VT]
	19	Plattsburgh [NY]
	20	Potsdam [NY]
	22	Ogdensburg [NY]
	23	Carthage [NY]
	24	Fulton [NY]

	25	Oswego [NY]
	26	Rome [NY]
	28	Auburn [NY]
	29	Newark [NJ]
	30	Sodus [NY]
	31	Geneva [NY]
Jan	1	Ithaca [NY]
	2	Owego [NY]

From the 1908 Diary of William A. Howell.

The Burliington Free Press and Times reported on December 7, 1908 that "Graustark" will be at The Strong theatre tomorrow afternoon and evening.

Miss Gertrude Perry appears as Princess Yetive; Alfred Britton as Grenfall Lorry, Harry Taylor as the comedian of the cast, John Burkell appears as Prince Bolaroz, Frank Howson appears as Prince Lorenze, Gladys Thorp plays Countess Dagmar, other artists are Miss Sadie Claflin, Miss Jane Lathin, William A. Howell and Norman Hillard.

KEENE.-OPERA HOUSE (A. W. Quinn, mgr.): ITEM: W. A. Howell of the Graustark co., will spend the holidays here with Mrs. Howell.

The New York Dramatic Mirror,
Saturday, December 26, 1908.

Terris C. Howard

WASHINGTON.
Summer Opera Thrives-
Graustark-The Columbia
Players-Theatrical News.

Washington.-May 10.-Graustark, with Gertrude Perry as the Princess Yetive and Alfred Britton as Greenfall Lorry, opens at the Academy of Music to a large audience, favorably impressed with this standard stage dramatization of George Barr McCutcheon's famous story. A notably proficient company includes H. O. Taylor, Edwin Melvin, W. A. Howell, Charles Doone, Frank Howson, Norman Millard, John Burkell, Susie Claflin, Jane Lothian, and Gladys Thorp. Next week, Rose Melville in Sis Hopkins.

john t. warde.
The New York Dramatic Mirror,
Saturday, May 15, 1909.

Sans Souci

The Sans Souci Hotel was located in the resort town of Cleverdale. New York on the shores of Lake George. It is very possible that this photograph may have been taken about December 3, 1908 as William A. Howell's diary indicates the play "Graustark" was performed in Glens Fall, New York on that date. They had played in Schenectady, New York the night before and Hoosick Falls, New York on December 4,1908.

Graustark cast relaxing at the Sans Souci hotel.
William A. Howell, 4th from the left.
(Photo from collection of Myra Van Haden).

The Graustark cast composed of Gertrude Perry as Princess Yetive, Allfred Britton as Grenfall Lary, Edwin Melvin as Baron Dangloss, H. O. Taylor as Harry Anguish, William A. Howell as Prince Gabriel, Gladys Thorp as Countess Dagmar, Jane Lothian as Aunt Yvonne and others.

Sans Souci

Possible cast pose from the play Graustark. William A. Howell
on the left and possibly Miss Gladys Thorp in the chair,
(Photo from collection of Terris C. Howard).

Louis James Tour

Louis James, a Shakespearean actor, and his wife Aphie James began their 1909- 1910 Annual Tour with Henry the VII and The Jealous Wife in Austin Texas at the Hancock Opera House on November 12, 1909. William A. Howell and others joined this tour group.

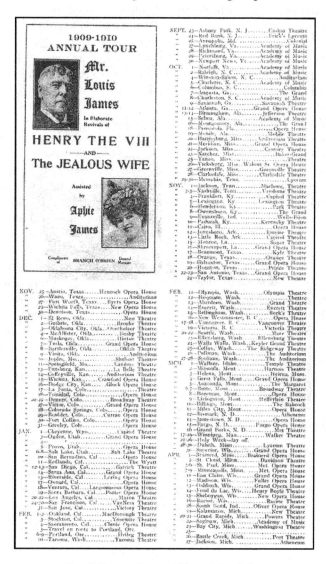

Louis James Annual Tour Schedule.
(From collection of Myra Van Haden).

Louis James Tour

Many newspapers during the Louis James tour reported on the performances given by members of the tour. Full copies of these newspaper articles are available on the internet, newspaper archives or the public library in that city.

A splendid performance of Shakespeare's "Henry the Eighth" was given at the Academy yesterday evening as reported by The Ledger Dispatch, Norfolk, Virginia on October 2, 1909. Louis James as Cardinal Wolsey, and Aphie James as Queen Katherine Otto F. Andrle as the Duke of Buckingham and William Howell, who played the King, merit special mention for their good work

The Nashville Tennessean reported on Wednesday morning November 3, 1909 that "Henry the Eighth" was presented at the Vendome on Tuesday night and a fine company of players consisting of Louis James in his favorite role as Cardinal Wosley, Mrs. James as Katherine the wife of the king, William Howell as the King and Otto Andrle as the Duke of Buckingham was stance a performance with none of the essentials lacking.

A great of Shakespeare's "Henry VIII" was reported by the Nashville Banner on November 3, 1909 at the Vendome with a great cast. Mr. Louis James as Wolsey, Queen Katherine and Henry VIII, played by William Howell.

The Kentucky Evening Gazette reported on November 6, 1909 that the matinee performance of "The Jealous Wife" was preceded with a scene from "Othello" presented by the Louis James Company. Aphie James appeared as Mrs. Oakley, Lois James as Mr. Oakley, William Howell as Charles Oakley, Otto Andrle as Major Oakley.

Shakespeare's play, "Henry VIII," according to the Beaumont Enterprise of Beaumont, Texas on November 18, 1909 at the Kyle Theatre was to an appreciative audience. The audience enjoyed the portrayal of the role of Cardinal Wolsey by Mr. James, Queen Katherine by Miss Aphie James, Mr. Otto P. Andrle in the roles of Buckingham and Cromwell, and William Howell, as the king who gave a very creditable performance.

The Standard of Ogden, Utah on January 4, 1910 reported that the Shakespearean actor, Louis James presented "The Merchant of Venice," to an appreciative audience at the Ogden Theater last evening. Louis James was great in the role of Shylock, Mrs. James as Portia, Ida Werner, Vera Walton, Otto Andrle, William Howell,-Edmund Flaig, Harrison Thompson, Hempstead Prince, and Richard Scott in their were very good.

A fair sized audience greeted the performance of "Henry Eighth at the Oxnard Opera House last night as reported by the Oxnard Courier, Oxnard, California on January 21, 1910. Mr. James was Cardinal Wolsey, Miss Aphie James was Queen Katherine, the part of Henry Eighth was well portrayed by William Howell and Otto F. Andrle was an ideal Buckingham.

The Oakland Tribune on February 2, 1910 announced that Henry VIII" with Louis James veteran Shakespearean actor, in the powerful role of Cardinal Wolsey, given at the Macdonough Theater. Aphie James, his wife appeared as Queen Katherine, William Howell as Henry VIII gave a good, though in no wise performance, and Otto F. Andrle as the Duke of Buckingham and later as Thomas Cromwell appeared to advantage in both roles.

Louis James and Aphie James, assisted by a most excellent company, presented Shakespeare's "Henry the Eighth" at the Clunie last night was reported by The Sacramento Star on February 5, 1910. Louis James portrayed Cardinal Wolsey and Miss Aphie James played Queen Catherine, William Howell was King Henry VIII and Otto F. Andrle was the Duke of Buckingham later as Thomas Cromwell

Louis James Tour

At the Theaters

"THE MERCHANT OF VENICE."

Shakespearean Drama in Six Acts Presented at the Bungalow.

CAST.

Duke of Venice	Harold Forrest
Antonio	Otto F. Andrle
Bassanio	Wm A. Howell
Gratiano	Edmund Flaig
Palanion	Harrison Thompson
Salarino	Hemstead Prince
Lorenzo	Richard I. Scott
Shylock	Louis James
Tubal	James Howe
Launcelot Gobbo	Paul Terhune
Old Gobbo	Le Roy Swaine
Balthazar	Henry Hempel
Portia	Aphie James
Nerissa	Ida Werner
Jessica	Vera Walton

WHILE it is conceded that one likes to see the new presentations of Louis James, it is further admitted that no season would seem complete without witnessing his portrayal of "Shylock," in "The Merchant of Venice." Mr. James' interpretation of this character is distinct and apart from the average conception of the role and for that reason is a revelation. The average layman conceives the money-lender as an old man, decrepit, bent and shaking with the weight of his years, malicious, sullen and totally abhorrent. As portrayed by Mr. James, the character assumes a virile strength of mind and body that is masterful. He gives us a new Shylock, a man in the prime of life, with red blood pounding in his veins, an eagle eye and firm step, a superior vigor and intelligence, whose personality dominates.

The Portia of Aphie James is a rare presentation of creative vital power and bespeaks the versatility of this charming actress. She infuse a charm and delicacy into her portrayal that won instant understanding.

"The Merchant of Venice" will be repeated today at evening and matinee performances, with "Henry VIII" again last night.

The Oregonian, Portland, Wednesday February 9, 1910.
(Permission to use granted by The Oregonian).

Louis James Tour

(Courtesy of the J. Willis Sayre-Carkeek Theatre Program Collection,
University of Washington Special Collections Library).

Louis James Tour

THREE NIGHTS AND TUESDAY MATINEE,
COMMENCING SUNDAY, EVENING, FEB. 20, 1910.

Sunday Evening and Tuesday Matinee

LOUIS JAMES

Assisted by

APHIE JAMES

In Shakespeare's

Henry the Eighth

(Edwin Booth Version)

THE CHARACTERS	THE PLAYERS
Cardinal Wolsey	Louis James
Henry the Eighth, King of England	William Howell
Cardinal Campeius	Richard I. Scott
Capucius	Thomas Reynolds
Duke of Buckingham	Otto F. Andrie
Duke of Norfolk	Paul Terhune
Duke of Suffolk	Harrison Thompson
Earl of Surrey	Hempstead Prince
The Lord Chamberlain	Edmund Flaig
Sir Thomas Lovell	Harold Forrest
Sir Henry Guildford	Le Roy Swaine
Thomas Cromwell	Otto F. Andrie
Gardiner	James Howe
Knevet, Surveyor to Buckingham	Arthur Robinson
Brandon	Henry Hempel
Queen Katharine, wife to Henry	Aphie James
Anne Bullen	Ida Werner
Patience	Vera Walton
Lady Denny	Louise Clarke

SYNOPSIS.

ACT FIRST—Scene 1st—Audience Chamber.
Scene Second—Street in London. Buckingham's Execution.
ACT SECOND—Same as Act First.
ACT THIRD—Blackfriars. Trial of Katharine.
ACT FOURTH—Same as Act First. Downfall of Wolsey.
ACT FIFTH—Queen's Apartment, Kimbolten. Death of Queen
Katharine.

LOVERA, A CIGAR OF THE DISCRIMINATING

PAGE THREE

(Courtesy of the J. Willis Sayre-Carkeek Theatre Program Collection,
University of Washington Special Collections Library).

Louis James Tour

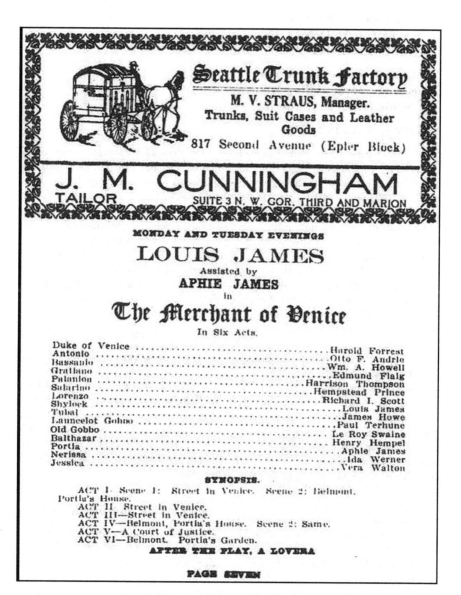

𝕾eattle 𝕿runk 𝕱actory

M. V. STRAUS, Manager.

Trunks, Suit Cases and Leather
Goods

817 Second Avenue (Epler Block)

J. M. CUNNINGHAM
TAILOR   SUITE 3 N. W. COR. THIRD AND MARION

MONDAY AND TUESDAY EVENINGS

LOUIS JAMES
Assisted by
APHIE JAMES
in

𝕿he 𝕸erchant of 𝕭enice
In Six Acts.

Duke of Venice	Harold Forrest
Antonio	Otto F. Andrie
Bassanio	Wm. A. Howell
Gratiano	Edmund Flaig
Palanion	Harrison Thompson
Salarino	Hempstead Prince
Lorenzo	Richard I. Scott
Shylock	Louis James
Tubal	James Howe
Launcelot Gobbo	Paul Terhune
Old Gobbo	Le Roy Swaine
Balthazar	Henry Hempel
Portia	Aphie James
Nerissa	Ida Werner
Jessica	Vera Walton

SYNOPSIS.
ACT I—Scene 1: Street in Venice. Scene 2: Belmont.
Portia's House.
ACT II—Street in Venice.
ACT III—Street in Venice.
ACT IV—Belmont, Portia's House. Scene 2: Same.
ACT V—A Court of Justice.
ACT VI—Belmont. Portia's Garden.
AFTER THE PLAY, A LOVERA

PAGE SEVEN

(Courtesy of the J. Willis Sayre-Carkeek Theatre Program Collection,
University of Washington Special Collections Library).

Louis James Tour

LOUIS JAMES SEEN AS THE CARDINAL IN "KING HENRY VIII"

Veteran Actor Makes Wolsey One of His Most Telling Roles — Aphie James as Katherine.

BY J. WILLIS SAYRE.

Louis James opened his annual engagement at the Moore last evening in one of the least known of the Shakespearean tragedies, "Henry VIII." Mr. James himself was re-sponsible for the last local presentation of the play, now eight years ago, so that it was a comparative novelty to those who assembled last night.

The tragedy tells a cheerless story, relieved only by the acting possibilities of three of its characters. Cardinal Wolsey, Queen Katherine and King Henry. The first two of those were in excellent hands last evening.

Although his opportunities are limited as compared with those afforded him in other classical roles, Louis James made much of the crafty cardinal. Advancing age seem only to mellow his art. His voice is as deep and resonant as ever, his reading both eloquent and musical, and his whole impersonation of marked impressiveness. He realizes the character as completely as this generation of playgoers will ever see it realized.

Aphie James' acting has been marked, season after season, by constant and notable improvement. In Mr. James' company she succeeds the late and great Polish actress, Modjeska, in the role of the queen, and is probably the youngest woman who has played Katherine on the American stage in decades. She showed to advantage in her two big scenes, the denunciation of the cardinal in the second act and in the death scene. Clear and most carefully measured enunciation is a feature of her entire impersonation.

William Howell was fair as the king. The remainder of the company, for the most part, was not equal to the demands put upon it.

Devoted followers of Shakespeare would do well to see Mr. James as Wolsey. The play is revived very infrequently, and this characterization is one of the best and most human in his extensive repertoire.

The [Seattle] Star, Monday, February 21, 1910.

Henry VIII

The Seattle Post-Intelligencer reported on February 21, 1910, that the cast of Louis James as Cardinal Wolsey, William Howell is Henry the Eighth, Otto Andrle as Thomas Cromwell, Aphie James as Queen Katherine and others presented Henry the Eighth at the Moore Theatre on Sunday Evening, February 20, 1910.

The Merchant of Venice

The Seattle Daily Times on Tuesday, February 1910, reported that the Louis James presented The Merchant of Venice at the Moore Theatre on Monday Evening. The cast consisted of Louis James as Shylock, Aphie James as Portia, William A. Howell as Bassanio. Otto F. Andrle as Antonio, Harold Forrest as the Duke of Venice and others.

The Merchant of Venice will be presented again this evening.

Experience

Opened October 24, 1914 in New York City.
Written by George V. Hobart and Produced by William Elliott.
Performed at the Booth, Casino and Maxine Elliott Theaters, New York City.
William Elliott as Youth, Frederick Perry as
Experience, William A. Howell as Work.

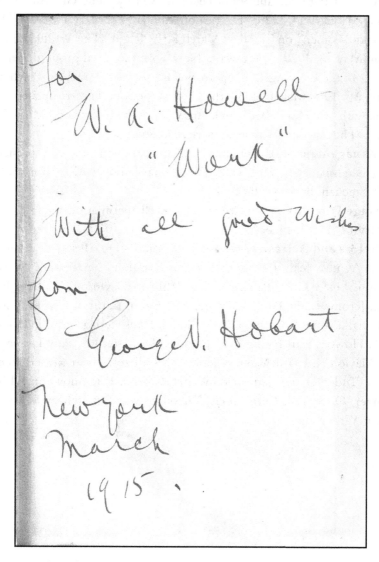

Autograph in front leaf of *Experience* by George V. Hobart, New York.
(From the collection of Terris C. Howard).

Los Angeles Repertory Theatre

1928/1929.

The Los Angeles Repertory Theatre opened its 1928-1929 season with "The Silver Cord" on Monday, November 19, 1928 at the Figueroa Playhouse at Figueroa and 9th Streets followed by "The Guardsman" on Monday, January 14, 1929; "Escape" on Monday, February 11, 1929; "The House of Women" on Tuesday, March 5, 1929 and "The World We Live In" on May 13, 1929. There was a New York theatrical group under the auspices of the Los Angeles Repertory Theatre at the Figueroa Playhouse during April and May. In 1930, the Civic Repertory Theatre opened their season with "And So to Bed" on January 27th at the Hollywood Music Box theatre. The personnel involved were as follows:

Management: L. E. Behymer, president; Simeon Gest, vice-president and general manager; H. Ellis Reed, secretary and production manager; H. O. Stechan, literary editor.

Stage Directors: John Cromwell, Lowell Sherman, Alfred Hickman, Paul Irving, H. Ellis Reed.

Actors and Actresses: 1929-1930 season: Barbjo Allen, Jean Altemus, Marie Aymes, Jean Buckley, Norman Cannon, Nora Ceil, Marion Clayton, Lester Cole, Patricia Craig, William Davidson, William Earl, Helen Jerome Eddy, Ruth Eldridge, Jane Elton, Kathryn Givney, Gloria Gottschalk, James F. Green, John Halloren, Hans Herbert, Phillip Homes, W. A. Howell, Paul Irving, Kay Johnson, Margaret Joy, Roy Lawrence, Elly Maylon, Edward Maynard, Betty Middleton, Tom Miller, Joseph North, Tudor Owen, Jan Reid, Wallis Roberts, Eric Snowdon, Phillip Stranger, Olive Tell, Carol Tevis, Theodore von Eltz, Jeffrey Williams, Barton Yarborough.

American Theatre Companies, 1888-1930.

Los Angeles Repertory Theatre

ORIGINAL CAST MEMBERS

The Repertory Theater production is fortunate in the presenting of three actors who were in the original cast in New York. Robert Edeson appears as the philosopher, which is the dominant role; Edgar Norton as that weird incarnation, the ichneumon fly, and Paul Irving in several effective impersonations. Mr. Irving is also the director of the production.

Edeson's death scene was notably forceful, and he was throughout exceptionally adequate. Norton ac-accomplished the grotesque most admirably. The Edeson role is difficult in that he is on stage through the entire action. Distinctly satisfying was the work of Barbara Jo Allen as the butterfly, Iris; Jane Reid, as Clythia, James F. Green and Jane Elton as the two beetles, with their amusing chirruping; W. A. Howell as the dictator in the ant scene. Irving supplied amusement both as butterfly and beetle, and did masterly rhythmic work as the counting ant. A charming bit was done by Patricia Craig in the final act as the moth born to die. This final act achieves beauty of a radiant sort.

Pilgrimage Play

Opened 9 July 1931.
Directed by Boyd Irwin.
Performed at the New Pilgrimage Play
Theatre, Hollywood, California.

Cast: **Ian Maclaren** as the Christ, **Anders Van Haden** as Pilate, **John Wagner** as Judas, **Ellis Reed** as Peter, **Doris Lloyd** as Mary Magdalene, **Lafayette McKee** as Calaphas, **George Gerwing** as the Demoniac.

HOLLAND ARTIST PLAYS PILATE IN BIBLICAL DRAMA

The Los Angeles Examiner on June 20, 1931 that other names have been added to the cast of the Pilgrimage Play, opening on July 9, will include Anders Van Haden for the part of Pilate, John Wagner to portray Judas Iscariot and H. Ellis Reed to the role of Apostle Peter. Anders Van Haden played with the Passion Players in Amsterdam.

ANDERS VAN HADEN IN PILGRIMAGE PLAY

Anders van Haden, noted stage and screen actor who plays a featured role in Fox's German "The Big Trail", will portray the part of Pilate in the Pilgrimage Play to be staged in Hollywood, July 9.

Unidentified newspaper article.

PILGRIM DRAMA STARTS TONIGHT

The Pilgrimage Play will be welcomed back tonight. Interrupted last season by the burning of the old playhouse the year before, the famous spectacle-drama will reopen in a new, concrete amphitheater.

Embodying in its construction the simple dignity of the architecture of Palestine 2000 years ago, the theater also combines every modern device of stage and equipment, electric lighting and convenience.

No less faithful than is the theater to the time and place of the drama's action is the scenic background that has been provided. Landscaped to resemble the natural scenery of Palestine, the grounds surrounding the playhouse have been planted with trees, shrubs and vines of the Holy Land.

The 100 players who will present the Pilgrimage Play through the limited season of the present summer have been selected from more than 1000 trained actors and actresses who offered their services.

Ian Maclaren internationally noted for his faithful portrayals of difficult roles, once more will take the part tomorrow night of the Christus. Myra Marsh, John Wagner, Anders van Haden and Walter Geer, have other leading roles.

Hollywood Daily Citizen,
Thursday, July 9, 1931.

Pilgrimage Play

The

Pilgrimage Play

"Life of the Christ"

As Transcribed and Produced
by
Christine Wetherill Stevenson

Presented Annually
in the
Pilgrimage Theatre
Hollywood

Eleventh Annual Season
1931

Los Angeles   ::   ::   California

(Program from the collection of Myra Van Haden).

Pilgrimage Play

Characters in the Play

Jesus of Nazareth..............Ian Maclaren
Judas Iscariot..................John Wagner
John the Beloved...............Walter Geer
Simon called Peter............H. Ellis Reed
James ....Clive Oliver
Matthew ....Howard Nugent
Philip ....Harold Mathews
Andrew ....Harold Nelson
Thomas ....Thomas Miller
Bartholomew ....Eric Snowden
Thaddeus ....James Welch
Simon the Cananaite.........Edward Wenig
James, son of Alpheus.........Rand Barker
Joseph ....Ambrose Barker
John the Baptist.............Richard Sterling
First Pharisee..................Boyd Irwin
Second Pharisee.............Barry Thomson
Third Pharisee.............George Elwin
Fourth Pharisee.............Edwin August
Simon the Sadducee..........Bram Nosson
An Old Shepherd...........Jeffrey Williams
Pilate ....Anders Van Haden
Scribe ....Clyde McCoy
Centurion ....Kenn Rendahl
Caiaphas ....Lafayette McKee
Blind Beggar.............Raymond Lawrence
Demoniac ....George Gerwing
Leper ....Alfred Aldridge
Nathaneal ....David Henderson
Sadducee ....Lafayette McKee
Second Sadducee.............George Gerwing
First Priest...................Wilbur Higby
Second Priest...............Richard Sterling
Third Priest ....George Elwin
Fourth Priest..............Robert Sherwood
Moses ....Kenn Rendahl
Elias ....Robert White
Rich Young Man..........Bern Boyd Irwin
Second Rich Young Man......Vernon Travis
Third Rich Young Man....Robert Sherwood
Lazarus ....Robert White
First Man ....Hal Price
Second Man.................Fred Cummings
Malchus ....Barry Thomson
Simon the Cyrenean.......Robert Underwood
Water Seller ....Ambrose Barker
Pandaira ....Kenn Rendahl
Money Changer............Fred Cummings
Wise Men.......... { James Welch / Harry Willard / Arthur Evers
Shepherds .... { Robert White / Bram Nosson / Robert Randall
Roman Soldiers...... { Bern Boyd Irwin / Robert Randall / Vernon Travis / Robert Sherwood

Jewish Soldiers...... { Edward Wolden / William Oakley
A Beggar ....John Steppling
Followers of Jesus... { Donald Murray / James Bartlett / Ernest Erskine / Jean DeJournette
Mary Magdalene...................Doris Lloyd
Mary, Mother of Jesus.........Myra Marsh
Samaritan Woman...........Belle Mitchell
Adultress ....Nancy Jackson
Martha ....Francesca Rotoli
Mary of Bethany..............Adda Gleason
First Woman of Bethany....Madoline Ashton
Second Woman of Bethany....Meeka Aldrich
Third Woman of Bethany.....Mildred Wheat
Mourning Women... { Doris Whitney / Lucille Young / Dorothy Woods
A Ragged Urchin.............Kathryn Pierce
Serving Woman to Caiaphas...Elizabeth Ross
Slave Boys.......... { Helen Benson / Mary Breen / Kathryn Pierce
Suzanna ....Belle Mitchell
Johanna ....Elizabeth Ross
Women of Bethany.. { Margaret Cummings / Alyse Kimball / Sally Melvor / Esther Hauschild / Estelle Wordette / Anne Gordon
Women of Jerusalem. { Margaret Steppling / Pauline Maclaren / Peggy Noy / Marilen Kay / Beryl LeBaron / Elaine St. Maur / Mary Breen / Gwen Moncrieff / Zena Vincent / Mary Ralston / Helen Stroup / Isabelle Belknap / Charlotte Sturgess / Estelle Goulding / Mary Alice Haines / Virginia Patterson / Dorothy France / Zillah Tancred
Children of Jerusalem { Elaine Shyleen / Lotus Correlli / May Lou Price / Violet Ohlman / Wendy Moncur
Serving Boy to Pilate.........Elaine Shyleen

Music by GERTRUDE ROSS .... Chorales by BACH
Disciples' Anthem at The Last Supper by DANE RUDHYAR

PILGRIMAGE PLAY QUARTETTE
Soprano—JESSIE MACDONALD PATTERSON
Contralto—ALMA LOWE CREIGHTON
Tenor—JOSEPH S. WAUGH
Bass—FRED C. McPHERSON

PILGRIMAGE PLAY DUO
Violin—SOL COHEN
Organ—MARGUERITE BITTER

Play Directed by BOYD IRWIN
Assistant Director, DON TRAVIS

ROY DAVIDSON ....Publicity
IDA MAY FRANK...........Charge of Tickets
LOUISE LYON.....Assistant, Charge of Tickets
CHARLEY PYKE ....Excursion
FRANK ALEXANDER ....Advertising
STELLA AVERY ....Secretary

ERNEST ERSKINE.............Stage Manager
EDDIE WOLDEN......Assistant Stage Manager
GEORGE SMITH............Director of Lights
HAROLD NAUMAN...........Chief Electrician
DALE JONES............ ....Stage Carpenter
CHARLES WHITING.......Master of Properties

ADELAIDE SCHUMAN ....Wardrobe

THE SILENT ERA

Some identification of the photographs and the movie stills from Biograph films has been made from the descriptions given by Robert M. Henderson in his book, D. W. Griffith, The Years at Biograph. Most of the other movie stills were previously identified. It should be noted that no credits were given for actors, actresses, or directors in the early silent films, especially those of Biograph.

The Biograph acting company went to Cuddebackville, New York. in late June of 1909 to film many of their productions and then returned to the studio in New York on July 4. They came back to Cuddebackville on July 26 and left again for New York on August 11. During this second stay at Cuddebackville, the film In Old Kentucky was completed. William A. Howell's daughter, Constance, was born in Monticello, which is located about 20 miles from Cuddebackville, on the same date. The Biograph acting company again returned to Cuddebackville on August 21. Another picture completed was Leather Stocking prior to returning to New York on August 30. It is fairly certain that those cast poses that I have identified are from the Cuddebackville filmed productions. The other cast poses that I have also identified as being filmed in Cuddebackville show the same buildings in the background, which could have been behind the Caudebec Inn. Marion Leonard and Mary Pickford worked for Biograph during this period. Gene Gauntier had also worked for Biograph for a short time before returning to Kalem.

Gene Gauntier worked at the Kalem Company with George Hollister, a cameraman, and Sidney Olcott. Olcott, Gauntier and Jack Clark (Gauntier's husband) left Kalem and formed their own company, the Gene Gauntier Feature Players. The Moving Picture World on December 21, 1912, announced the formation of the Gene Gauntier Feature Players Company, that will release its productions through Warner's Features. It has been noted the Gene Gauntier Feature Players Company was located in Jacksonville, Florida during the production of their films.

William Howell made several pictures with the Gene Gauntier Feature Players. Those have been fairly easy to identify as the film stills are identified on the back or there was a Warner's Features press release like the Keystone Press release for False Evidence.

The next sequence of films presented are those where William Howell supported Marion Leonard with films produced by the Rex studios. A review of Thru Flaming Gates from The Motion Picture Story Magazine and the photos are from the original film stills are representative of that era. The End of the Circle photograph is from an advertising postcard used in those times to promote the coming of a film to a local theatre.

William A. Howell worked also for the Thanhouser Film Corporation in the Falstaff and Arrow productions from 1915 through early 1916. There are a few film stills of his directing and acting efforts with Thanhouser. He left Thanhouser in 1916 and went to Miami to work for the C. C. Field Motion Picture Company and Field Feature Film Company.

Towards the end of World War I, William A. Howell made several patriotic shorts and examples of those circulars used for promoting Our Flag, Columbia and The Star Spangled Banner are presented. The Star Spangled Banner was photographed by the same George K. Hollister who had worked earlier with Gene Gauntier.

Other films directed by William A. Howell were Home Sweet Home and Jesus of Nazareth.

Unidentified studio stills are included as I have been unable to identify the films or the actors and actresses except for William A. Howell.

The Silent Era
1920 Motion Picture Studio Directory

Directors

HOWELL, W. A.: b Cincinnati, O., 1877; previous to screen career, dramatic actor, director, producer; since 1910 organizer of own independent picture producing companies; specializes in comedies. Office, 110 West 42d st., N. Y. C.; Bryant 4527.

1921 Motion Picture Studio Directory

Directors

HOWELL, W. A.: b Cincinnati, O., 1877; screen career, director, producer; since 1910 organizer of independent picture producing companies. William A. Howell Prod. Office, 703 Market st., San Francisco, Calif.

William A. Howell Movie Still from an unidentified movie.
(Photo from the collection of Myra Van Haden).

The Politician's Love Story
Biograph - 22 February 1909.
Directed by D.W. Griffith.

Cast: **Mack Sennett, Linda Arvidson, Frank Powell, William A. Howell**.

A contemporary comedy filmed in Central Park, New York City in mid-January, 1909.

Mack Sennett and William A. Howell.
(Photo from collection of Myra Van Haden).

The Voice of the Violin
Biograph - 13 March 1909.
Directed by D. W. Griffith.

Cast: **Marion Leonard, Arthur Johnson, Donald Crisp, David Miles, William A. Howell** as a Violin Player.

"**Voice of the Violin.**"-A Biograph picture which ought to command attention from critical audiences and which is lively enough to attract any one. A music master, rejected by an heiress, joins a band of anarchists. He is one of two selected by lot to blow up the home of a hated capitalist. While watching outside the door he hears a violin playing one of his compositions. He discovers from this that it is the home of the girl he loves. He rushes to the cellar where his confederate is about to light the fuse on the fatal bomb. He tries to prevent it, but is overpowered, bound and left to share the fate of the inmates of the house. He struggles violently and succeeds in biting the fuse in two before the bomb is ignited. He is found shortly after, taken up stairs, and the ending is happy enough to suit the most exacting. The acting is good, the staging could scarcely be better, and interest is maintained to the end. This film should have a long run.

Moving Picture World, March 20, 1909. p. 337.

Donald Crisp pointing and William A. Howell on stage.
(Photo from collection of Myra Van Haden).

In Old Kentucky
Biograph - 1909.
Directed by D. W. Griffith.

Cast: **Mary Pickford, Henry Walthall, Owen Moore Kate Bruce, Frank Powell, William A. Howell** as a Rebel.

A Civil War melodrama filmed in Cuddebackville located in the Orange Mountains of New York.

Cast pose with William A. Howell and possibly Owen Moore.
(Photo from collection of Myra Van Haden).

In Old Kentucky

Two brothers George and Robert enlist on opposite sides in the Civil War. Robert is captured as a spy for the South, but escapes and hides in his parents' house. George leads the search party, but doesn't reveal his brother's hiding place, and Robert escapes. After the war, George is a hero and Robert is down on his luck. George cautiously welcomes him back into the family home.

Cast pose with William A. Howell at far left.
(Photo from collection of Myra Van Haden).

Leather Stocking - Biograph - 1909.
Directed by D. W. Griffith.

This is possibly the cast of *"Leather Stocking"* also filmed in Cuddebackville, New York.

Cast pose with William A. Howell in the Indian costume.
(Photo from collection of Terris C. Howard).

Unidentified Biograph Films

**Cast pose with William A. Howell at the far left.
(Photo from collection of Myra Van Haden).**

**Cast pose of William A. Howell.
(Photo from collection of Terris C. Howard).**

False Evidence
Warner's Features, Inc. - 1911.
Directed by Gene Gauntier.

Cast: **Gene Gauntier** as Florence Cobb, **Harry Gsell** as Jack Ainsley, **William A. Howell** as Richard Hunt.

FALSE EVIDENCE
(IN THREE PARTS)
A Powerful Melodrama
FEATURING
GENE GAUNTIER
Released by Warner's Features, Inc.

"Don't Hit Me. I've Suffered Enough."

WILL BE SHOWN AT

Unidentified, unidentified, Gene Gauntier and William A. Howell. (Program from collection of Myra Van Haden).

False Evidence

William Howell upper left and stage center below.

False Evidence

False Evidence

FALSE EVIDENCE
(IN THREE PARTS)

Released by Warner's Features, Inc.

A Superb Dramatic Story of Love, Hate, Revenge and Remorse, Interpreted by Gene Gauntier and a Stellar Cast.

Miss Gene Gauntier has scored another dramatic triumph in "False Evidence," a human interest story of unusual strength. She is ably assisted in this three-part Warner's Feature by W. A. Howell, Harry Gsell and a clever child actress.

John Ainsley, Sr., at his death, unable to make provision for his son, Jack, exacts from his more fortunate business partner a promise that he will take care of the lad. In accord with his pledge, Morris Cobb sends for the youth at the completion of the latter's college term.

Jack then enters upon a business career with the firm of Cobb & Company, and promptly falls in love with his benefactor's daughter, Florence, much to the chagrin of Richard Hunt, business manager for Cobb & Company, also a suitor of the girl.

Hunt is an unscrupulous adventurer, but he has managed to hide his defalcations and forgeries. Jack's activities and quick perception however, cause him grave apprehension.

At a ball given at the home of Cobb, Florence receives two proposals; one from Hunt, which she rejects; the other from Jack Ainsley. The latter leaves that night as the accepted suitor.

Hunt is goaded by jealousy and hatred, and determines to rid himself of so formidable and dangerous a rival. He introduces Jack at his club, and readily advances money to him on his personal notes.

To recoup his losses, Jack becomes a nightly habitue of the gambling palace. At the end of his resources and pressed by Hunt for payment, Jack is obliged to give in exchange for his debts a valuable Saracon ring. Hunt sees to it that Florence is made acquainted with Jack's habits and precarious finances. Therefore when a robbery and assault is committed by Hunt, the circumstantial evidence is subtly made to point conclusively to Jack. Florence is rudely awakened when she finds Jack's Saracon ring on the scene of the crime, and is convinced of her lover's perfidy and guilt.

In withholding the ring during Jack's trial, as an act of delicacy, Florence unwittingly robs the defence of its only tangible evidence to prove his innocence.

The unravelling of the plot however, moves speedily to a happy conclusion once the girl has the right key to the situation. In the end, guilt is punished and love is triumphant.

Here is a photoplay that will hold the interest of man, woman or child—and hold it triumphantly to the end. SEE IT!

KEYSTONE PRESS, NEW YORK.

Movie programs were usually provided at a minor cost to the silent movie customers so they could follow plot and action of the movie.

False Evidence

William A. Howell, Gene Gauntier, unidentified, and Marion Leonard.
(Photo from collection of Myra Van Haden).

Unidentified, William A. Howell, Gene Gauntier.
(Photo from collection of Myra Van Haden).

Gene Gauntier Feature Players

Gene Gauntier

For the Past Five Years Premier Leading Lady of the

KALEM COMPANY

Begs to Announce

That She Will in Future Appear ONLY With

The Gene Gauntier

Feature Players

Supported by	Under the Direction of
Jack J. Clark	**Sidney Olcott**

Films Will Be Distributed EXCLUSIVELY Through

Warner's Features

The Moving Picture World, December 21, 1912.

Twilight
Gene Gauntier Feature Players - 1912.
Distributed by Essanay Film Manufacturing Company
Directed by Gene Gauntier.

Cast: **Francis X. Bushman, Martha Russell, Harry Mainhall, Ruth Stonehouse, William A. Howell**.

Francis X. Bushman, William A. Howell and Gene Gauntier.
(Photo from collection of Myra Van Haden).

TWILIGHT

GENE GAUNTIER FEATURE PLAYERS
519 W. 54TH STREET
NEW YORK CITY

(Inscription on back on photograph)

Twilight
Gene Gauntier Feature Players – 1912.
Distributed by Essanay Film Manufacturing Company
Directed by Gene Gauntier.

"**TWILIGHT**" (Essanay), Sept. 6.–Francis X. Bushman and Martha Russell present a most tender and sympathetic portrayal of a retrospect, brought back to them by reason of the engagement of their granddaughter. Harry Mainhall and Ruth Stonehouse carried the parts of the young lovers.

The Moving Picture World, September 21, 1912.

Gene Gauntier and William A. Howell.
(Photo from collection of Myra Van Haden).

GENE GAUNTIER FEATURE PLAYERS
519 W. 54TH STREET
NEW YORK CITY

(Inscription on back on photograph)

She of the Wolf's Breed
Gene Gauntier Feature Players – 1912.
Distributed by Essanay Film Manufacturing Company
Directed by Gene Gauntier.

Cast: **Gene Gauntier, William A. Howell.**

William A. Howell, unidentified and Gene Gauntier.
(Photo from collection of Myra Van Haden).

She of the Wolf's Breed
GENE GAUNTIER FEATURE PLAYERS.
519 W. 54TH STREET
NEW YORK CITY

(Inscription on back on photograph)

The Defender of the Name
Rex - 18 January 1912.
Directed by Stanner E. V. Taylor.

Cast: **Marion Leonard** as John's sister, **William A. Howell** as a Southern gentleman.

REX.

THE DEFENDER OF THE NAME (Jan. 28).- John Potter is the son of one of the most distinguished and courageous families in old Virginia. The stirring news that Sumpter had been fired upon volleys its pregnant purport into the homes of the South. John volunteers to serve. Disguised as a Union soldier, John starts on his mission of securing the Union forces' plans. As he steals through the Union lines he comes upon a squad of Union soldiers, and in their midst a Confederate spy. A sharp order and from the barrels of twelve guns the prisoner's punishment is meted out to him. Like a blow it dawns upon John that, if detected, that would be his fate. His courage fails him and he turns toward the Confederate lines. He runs to his home, and bursts in upon his sister, who alone is awake. A few brief words and she knows all. The boy, desperate in his shame, runs into another room; there a muffled shot-a thin wreath of smoke tells its grim tale. She determines to accomplish her brother's mission.

She manages to get into the Union lines, secures the plans and when she reaches home, where her dead brother lies, she places the plans in his pocket. The Confederates find him and he is buried with military honors.

The Moving Picture World, February 3, 1912.

Independent.

"THE DEFENDER OF THE NAME" (Rex), January 28 - A wartime picture some of whose scenes have more than usual grace and charm. These are mostly well lighted and well-stage interiors. It is not a convincing story in spite of its being very well acted; but there are in it some emotional moments. A Southern officer is sent on a dangerous mission; but becomes panic-stricken and takes refuge in his home. His sister (Miss Leonard) tries to waken in him some sense of duty; but he is so crazy that he goes into the next room and commits suicide. The girl goes across into enemy's lines gets the information needed (it is a paper) and then, placing it in her dead brother's hand, drags him out where the sentries will find him. She thus defends the name from shame. The photographs are excellent, the film of full length and it will make a feature. It should be advertised as Miss Marion Leonard's picture.

The Moving Picture World, February 24, 1912.

THE DEFENDER OF THE NAME.

Without wanting to be unkind, we wish that the producers would forget the American Wars. There are other campaigns on record (though, to judge by the picture theatres, one might be inclined to doubt it), and one fancies that many historical battles would be of greater interest to an English audience, and afford quite as much scope for spectacular display as that everlasting, inevasible American Civil War, which is the period selected for at least every second battle film one sees. In the first place, it is to be doubted whether the average Englishman had ever taken the slightest interest in this eternal campaign before the picture theatres came to harp upon it so incessantly, and, secondly, there is no question that, as regards costume and incident, it is one of the dullest, most unromantic affairs on record. The French Revolution is a far more prolific period for the dramatist; practically every American War picture could be transported to France with a little ingenuity and gain immeasurably thereby. In making this protest, we are not trying to quarrel with the present film in general, "The Defender of the Name" is an excellent little drama, and it contains many really sensational moments, but, to our mind at any rate, it would have a considerably stronger appeal if its producer had opened a new page in his history book. He tells how the son of a family, entrusted with an important mission, turns coward at the critical moment and shoots himself, leaving the completion of his task to his brave little sister who successfully accomplishes it and thus saves the honour of their name. If a wee bit "stagey" and, as a whole, carries conviction. It is admirably mounted and cleverly photographed. It will doubtless prove much to the taste of the average audience. (Rex film. Released June 15th. Length 1,000 ft.)

The Bioscope, May 9, 1912.

The End of the Circle
Rex - 25 February 1912.
Directed by Stanner E. V. Taylor.

Cast: **Marion Leonard** as the mother, **William A. Howell** as the husband.

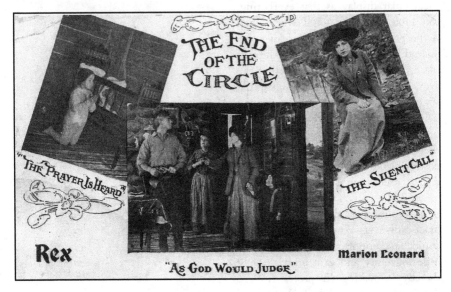

Center photograph: William A. Howell, unidentified,
Marion Leonard, unidentified.
(Postcard from collection of Myra Van Haden).

REX.

THE END OF THE CIRCLE (Feb. 25). - Discouraged and disheartened with her uncompromising poverty and the narrow prospects for improving the bleak conditions, she goes away with another. It was hard to leave the little tot and the husband vainly struggling against the relentless tide of invincible circumstance.

In the lonesome night the child prays for the mother-woman, and across the dreary waste of desert life she hears the call-and heeds. The telepathic tie that binds the child's mind to her own transmits the wistful message, and the mother-heart conquers. The nebulous shadow of night and blight departs; the withered hope buds and blooms away, and she takes the narrow path back to those to whom her life is consecrated.

The Moving Picture World, February 24, 1912.

The End of the Circle

The example shown above and on the preceding page represent
the postcards that were used to promote silent films.
(Postcard from collection of Myra Van Haden).

Through Flaming Gates
Rex - 3 March 1912.
Directed by Stanner E. V. Taylor or Edwin S. Porter.

Cast: **Marion Leonard** as Katherine Norton, **William A. Howell** as Dr. John Norton.

Marion Leonard, unidentified, and William A. Howell.
(Photo from collection of Myra Van Haden).

William A. Howell, unidentified, Marion Leonard, unidentified.
Unidentified, William A. Howell.
(Photos from collection of Myra Van Haden).

Through Flaming Gates

 # Thru Flaming Gates
(Rex)

By HENRY ALBERT PHILLIPS

"JOHN"—Mrs. Norton turned from the mirror to look at her husband—"you're keeping in mind that dance at the Emerys' tonight? It's time you began to dress."

"I was on the point of speaking to you about it, Katherine. I'm sorry, but I cant go."

"Cant go!" His wife wheeled around with an angry flush.

"No, Katherine," he said quietly, "and I repeat, dear, I'm sorry."

"Well, that wont be a sufficient excuse for Mrs. Emery—nor me, either. Why cant you go?"

The man gave a warning glance from his wife to the child who sat talking to her doll in the corner. "Here, Toddles," he said, kindly, "take your doll into the parlor, and let her play a tune on the piano."

The child sprang up and obeyed, delighted with this unasked-for privilege.

"Now, Katherine, we can talk. I dont like to have the child hear sharp words between us. I cant go to this dance because my duties as house-surgeon in the hospital wont permit it, tonight at least."

"Then why didn't you tell me before this?" snapped the angry woman, flouncing across the room. "Because, until this

moment, I couldn't bear to refuse you, dear. Then I remembered that Dr. Harrison would not be in attendance tonight."

"If he could get off, why couldn't you?"

"There is a delicate piece of work to be done tonight — the patient is mine."

"A woman, I suppose!"

"Katherine! I——" He had raised his voice, but now said drily, "No, a child, about the age of our little Toddles. Once she was just as pretty, until fire disfigured her sweet face. Her life is still in danger. Enough live skin grafted on her poor little burned face will do it. See, Katherine," he slipped up his sleeve above his elbow and disclosed a flaming square of healing flesh. "I shall contribute another piece as large as this tonight."

"I wish I'd never married a doctor, and have no chance for pleasure in life at all," she pouted.

"None!" he asked, wounded. "So Toddles and I—" He choked slightly. "Oh, Katherine, if you would only think before you speak —you're like a spoiled child."

"Well, I'm going to the dance tonight, anyway," she retorted, biting her nails.

97

(Courtesy G. Duclow Theatre Collection, Free Library of Philadelphia).

Through Flaming Gates

"And Toddles?" There was a sinister note in the man's voice. "Remember, the maid wont be back tonight."

"I guess if she can be put to bed and left when we are out a while together, she can be put to bed tonight." She rose and moved to the mirror and began to attend to her toilet again.

"I shan't be treated like a child," she protested, "nor a slave, either. Toddles. come in and be undressed."

"Toddles aint 'fraid 'tay 'lone. You tin leave Toddles, Nannah."

The bravado faded from the woman again. Then she undressed the child in stolid silence. She put Toddles and her doll to bed, and then took a seat before the fire, the rebel-

"Katherine," said the doctor, rising and putting on his coat, "I'm on the verge of being disappointed in you. Still, I dont believe—I cant believe it—that you'll go without Toddles and me!"

He kissed her impassive brow and left the house.

She paused and thought, for a moment, a wave of fear passing thru her slender frame. Then she caught sight of her own pretty face in the mirror and made her decision.

lion in her heart only evidenced by an occasional sigh. Soon she found herself following the ravishing movements of a waltz being played by some one next door. When it was finished she rose, determinedly. "Oh. I must go—for a little while—just this once. I must!"

She left Toddles asleep, a smile on her pretty face, the doll clasped close to the little heart that was coming, day after day, to long more and more for a mother's love.

Through Flaming Gates

Twenty minutes later she was the center of a merry group of laughing and chatting friends at the Emerys'. The house was like a fairy palace, lit with hundreds of lights and with the most delightful music stealing thru the place from a great bank of palms, where the orchestra was hidden. Some of the bitterness of the little domestic unpleasantness still tainted her enjoyment of it all. "It takes young physicians so long to rise to the point where their wives can be somebody," she was thinking, when a mellifluous male voice broke into her revery.

"What, Kathy! Well, this is a pleasant surprise!" The newcomer, a large man, with a heavy mustache and an air of familiarity, seized her hand and held it, as tho he had some right to it. He had had, years ago. Katherine and he were once engaged. "Where's John?" he continued, looking around among the gay throng.

"He—he couldn't come."

"So that's why you stand here looking like a funeral, eh? Well, dry those tears now—and I see it's up to me to do the honors. How about this waltz?" He bowed gallantly and held out his arm.

"It is yours!" she said, gaily, and laying her pretty, white-gloved hand on his shoulder, they were soon whirling about the dazzling room, all else forgotten but the dance.

"Oh, that was glorious!" she cried, flushed and bright-eyed with excitement, when they had taken seats.

"There's more where that came from," he said, still holding the dainty hand and gazing down at her with old-time admiration. "Come, let's have the whole of the next one." They took the floor again.

"By the way, Frank," she said, as it suddenly occurred to her for the first time, "where's your wife? I've been looking about for her."

"Oh, you wont find her, because she isn't here." She thought he held her just a little tighter here, as if in assurance. It was indeed an exquisite waltz.

"Not sick, I hope?" she inquired.

"An attack of the sillies, that's all. She gets 'em often. Sometimes I'm thankful"—a little pressure of the hand this time. "The cook's kid, or granddaughter, or something, was going to have something done to it up at the hospital. So, of course, Millie had to go with the cook to the hospital. Did you ever hear anything so silly? Kid was badly burned, or something of the kind. Why, what the deuce is the matter, Kathy?"

The woman had stopped dead still, her face gone pale, her body trembling.

"Escort me to a seat," she said, thickly. A sudden dread had come over her of she knew not what, a sudden lofty veneration, too, for this woman whose sympathy was so great that she could forego pleasures such as this.

"What's it all about?" her escort was demanding.

"Why, John is the surgeon performing this grafting operation tonight on the cook's child!"

"Ho, ho, ho!" roared the man, noisily. "If that isn't a rich coincidence! Millie and John spending the evening together at the hospital—Kathy and Frank doing the same here—at the dance!"

"At the dance," murmured the woman over and over again. "We're enjoying *ourselves*, and they're trying to make others happy!"

"But they're enjoying themselves just as much"—he glanced at the woman's unhappy countenance—"perhaps more than we are. That's their way—this is ours."

"I wish to God it were mine!"

"Tut, tut! Sit down here, before this cheerful grate fire, and we'll have a cozy chat."

She seated herself, drawing away from him with a shudder he did not notice.

"Come, come, Kathy, brace up. This isn't a bit like you." He shook the arm of the preoccupied woman.

"Look!" she cried in a voice of almost tragedy, pointing toward a glowing coal that had tumbled from the grate and rolled to the very edge

(Courtesy G. Duclow Theatre Collection, Free Library of Philadelphia).

Terris C. Howard

Through Flaming Gates

of the tiling. A little blue flame curled in a circle and licked the edge of the flooring.

"Oh, that's easily settled." He rose and brushed back the venomous firebrand with his heel. "It's a good thing we came here."

"If we hadn't?" She leaned forward tensely, her eyes filled with a terrible anxiety that saw only a room in a little frame cottage on the other side of the town, where a sweet-faced, neglected child lay alone, hugging a rag doll to her heart, and in the adjoining room was an open fire, like this. Then the image became blurred by a red glare.

"Well, if we hadn't," the man was saying, as tho obscured from her by smoke and with a voice muffled as tho by crackling flames, "it might have been a case of 'produce the policy!' You must be ill, Kathy." He was scanning her pale face and straining eyes. She rose unsteadily.

"I must go home," she whispered.

"So here's where you hide, is it?" cried a cheery voice from behind them.

"Oh, is that you, Mr. and Mrs. Emery?" responded Katherine's escort. "Mrs. Norton had a little turn during the dance, so we decided to sit it out."

"But I simply must have one dance!" protested Mr. Emery, good-naturedly. "You cant very well refuse your host, you know. Emily, you run along with Frank."

Katherine looked up helplessly into the fun-loving face of her new companion. There seemed no way out of it.

"Just one," she said, weakly, and they slipped out into the maze of whirling dancers. But to the heavy-hearted woman this was a dance of death. All that sea of bobbing faces reflected but one vision in her eyes— that of a little child, some relative of

(Courtesy G. Duclow Theatre Collection, Free Library of Philadelphia).

Anders Van Haden

Through Flaming Gates

a cook, with a face all scared and distorted.

She was now being carried, almost a dead weight, in the arms of her partner. Once it seemed to her that that burned image was—she tried to wipe away the horrid vision along with the cold drops on her forehead— the scarred face of Toddles. Her heart leaped with a new feeling, yet sweet in its agony. But the insistent call of frivolity in her nature was not yet quite stilled.

Suddenly she stiffened and stood still for the second time, her head bent forward, listening. "You heard it?" she asked, dazedly.

"What?" asked her partner, in amazement.

"The fire bell!"

"Why, that was the notes of the triangle running thru the waltz. Come, we may as well finish it—we're near the end."

And they started out heavily again.

The woman still swayed, tho perhaps for the last time in her life, by weakness. A voice was growing stronger every minute in her singing ears, the voice of her own child, calling, calling. And a new voice in response in her heart was gaining volume and steeling her will and limbs to a deed of strength. And when the distant notes of the fire alarm floated again, above the music, the laughter, the gaiety, this time piercing her heart with the keen blade of remorse, she broke rudely from her partner and fled from the ball-room, roughly flinging aside all in her path. Thus Mrs. Norton lost her place in society for all time—and the dance went on!

But outside, running thru the cold, gas-lit streets of a winter's midnight, with hair streaming, white neck and shoulders cruelly bared to the blast, and the futile cry of a mother's breaking heart on her lips, was the woman who had turned from the

(Courtesy G. Duclow Theatre Collection, Free Library of Philadelphia).

Terris C. Howard

Through Flaming Gates

vanities of life to its duties, seemingly too late.

For thru the midnight stillness droned the dismal clangor of several fire apparatus, wearily making their way homeward, and in the eastern sky was the faint glow of a dying conflagration. All that was left of the Norton cottage was a tottering chimney, four broken foundation walls and an ugly mass of smoking ruins!

The desultory group of spectators who remained were watching, with morbid curiosity, several firemen, who still poked about among the ruins in an evidently hopeless search for what the fire should have left of a tragedy. The crowd was startled by a blood-freezing cry that at first seemed to rise from the midst of the steam and smoke. It was some time before they discerned a wild female figure, clothed in spattered and bedraggled silk, hugging a half-charred object close to her half-bared breast with one hand, while the other was extended before her, the fingers crooked stiffly in appeal.

Several men rushed to her side and charitably threw a warm blanket over her icy shoulders.

All the while she laughed mirthlessly, while great, meaningless tears flowed down her cheeks. Then they looked into her eyes and saw that the light of reason had departed from them!

And all the way to the hospital she continued to laugh and point to the charred rag doll, a smudge against her fair white breast, murmuring in a harsh voice, "See! I found her— my Toddles! Never shall she leave mother's breast again—*my baby!*"

And some men wept that night to whom tears had for years been strangers.

It must have been fully two hours before this when Dr. Norton had finished the first tedious stage of skin-grafting in the case of a wan little child. His assistant beckoned him aside.

"You're wanted."

"I cant come," was his reply.

"There's been a fire."

"My God! any more of this?" He pointed to the prostrate figure.

"They're calling for you again, out there in the receiving ward."

Dr. Norton, still in his ghostly operating garb, flitted sinisterly toward a cot on which lay a little creature, sobbing as if her heart would break. The man gave a sharp cry and ripped the coverlet from the bed, disclosing a nightgown with a few holes burned in it.

"Toddles! My little Toddles!" he moaned, scanning every inch of the white flesh.

"But, daddy, I lost dolly—wanta go home!" the child sobbed.

He folded her in his arms, and then turned on a fireman, demanding, "And Mrs. Norton—tell me—oh, my God, you *must* have saved her! I tell you, you must have!"

"They're lookin'—now. But I'm afraid——" The man stopped.

"Here, orderly! My coat and hat —and our ambulance! Oh, Katherine, Katherine! to think that I spoke one cross word! That I suspected you of—— What does the child say?"

"I tay," repeated Toddles, laboredly, "I tole my Nannah she tood doe—an' I 'tay home wid dolly. I want dolly!"

"The soulless wretch!" muttered the doctor, half reeling under this new intelligence. Then he turned fiercely on the assembled group. "Go! Leave me with my child! I want to be alone—oh, I want to be alone!"

And they left him, a crumpled heap, dry sobs shaking his broad shoulders, the curly head of his sleepy child nestled close to his face.

"Will Nannah tome toon?" she was saying, drowsily.

When they brought "Nannah" in, what seemed years later to all concerned, and gently laid her on a warm, white sheet, she was calmer and laughing softly now.

Some one whispered in his ear, "Come," and he followed mechanically. His pain-wearied eyes saw

(Courtesy G. Duclow Theatre Collection, Free Library of Philadelphia).

Through Flaming Gates

nothing until they looked into those of his wife. In that moment he saw it all, and his big heart opened wide with pity, with contrition, with love, with sorrow.

"Toddles — mother's Toddles!" Katherine was whispering softly.

"Waken the child," said the doctor to the orderly. "We must act quickly. If this is a temporary aberration, perhaps we can cure it. Exposure has accentuated it. Bring stimulants and get her warm. Hurry!" He turned to the child. "Mother has come, dear. She is calling to you. Speak to her."

The child climbed on the cot and nestled on her mother's breast.

"Nannah — Toddles been talling and talling and talling 'oo!"

The woman stopped her mumbling and looked at the little creature with startled, puzzled eyes. She turned her head one side to drink in the childish voice. Then she drew the miserable remnant of a doll from beneath the clothes and looked from it to the nestling child. Then she closed her eyes wearily, and when she reopened them the rag doll dropped from her fingers. And ever so gently her hands stole round and enwrapped the little one to her breast. Then she bent her face, half fearfully, as tho she feared it were all a myth, toward the curly head. The sobbing man, just above them, could hear her whispered words, "My precious little Toddles—mother has had a terrible, terrible dream! Come, let us sleep till your dear old daddy comes back from the hospital. Precious, precious Toddles!"

But Toddles was cooing over a half-charred rag doll.

"Nannah, oo bringed Toddles her dolly back. Nighty-night, Nannah, nighty-night!"

(Courtesy G. Duclow Theatre Collection, Free Library of Philadelphia).

71

A Scrap of Paper
Kinemacolor – 1913.

The Kinemacolor Company was a pioneer firm specializing in natural color films in the Jacksonville, Florida area. Kinemacolor was dependant on the overseas markets that were cut off by World War I and they relied on a special cumbersome projector for the projection of its films. These factors and the uneconomical Kinemacolor process led to their decline. William A. Howell worked for this studio on "A Scrap of Paper" and the following "All Rivers meet at the Sea."

"A SCRAP OF PAPER"
(Kinemacolor).

The Kinemacolor studios are again fortunate in the working out of an entertaining light comedy, one of the most difficult stories to handle. The vogue runs much to dramas and knockabout farces, but this is possibly due to the fact that no general effort has been made to develop the less strenuous phase of the comedy. "A Scrap of Paper" has to do with the love affairs of a French demoiselle. It is worth notice that the Kinemacolor interior scenes (this reel is one of the few that are set indoors) have an immense advantage over the black and white. The color scheme gives the stage settings warmth and an illusion of realism that is lacking in the colorless films.

Rush.

Variety, Friday, March 28, 1913.

All Rivers Meet at the Sea
Broncho – 2 Jul 1913.

"ALL RIVERS MEET AT THE SEA" (Broncho), July 2. - A Story of love and jealousy. The moving picture man appears in a stage wedding and then later surprises the company by really marrying the leading lady. The envious lover knocks him off the yacht on their wedding trip. He is rescued by fisherman, but his mind is a blank. From this point the plot becomes very obvious and loses strength accordingly. The villain falls in the sea at the close of the picture when husband and wife are reunited.

The Moving Picture World, July 2, 1913, p. 50.

The Boss
William A. Brady Picture Plays, Inc. - 24 May 1915.
Directed by Emile Chautard and
produced by William A. Brady.
Distributed by World Pictures Corp.

Cast: **Alice Brady** as Emily Griswold, **Holbrook Blinn** as Michael Regan, **Charles F. Abbe** as James Griswold, **Bert Starkey** as Porky McCoy, **William Marion** as Archbishop Sullivan, **Julia Stuart** as Mrs. Regan, **William A. Howell**.

Variety: 14 May 1915, p. 19.

Note: World Film Corporation also produced films in Jacksonville, Florida. World released several other Florida made productions during this period with Holbrook Blinn and Alice Brady.

Holbrook Blinn, unidentified, unidentified, and William A. Howell at far right. (Photo from collection of Myra Van Haden).

The Boss

Drama/Social. With the $1,000 prize money that wharf rat Michael Regan wins boxing, he is able to purchase a saloon and a freight-handling concern and begins his rise to success. By persuading his men to work for half the standard rate, Regan gains control of grain-shipping contracts held by his rival, the once wealthy James Griswold, now on the verge of bankruptcy because of Regan. When Regan meets and falls in love with Emily Griswold, he offers to merge with Griswold for permission to court Emily. She marries Regan, but remains a wife in name only. When Griswold's son provokes a strike, Regan's friend, Porky McCoy, hits the young Griswold with a brick as he make a speech. Regan is arrested as an instigator, but McCoy's wife insists that her husband confess. In prison, Regan turns over his property to Emily and releases from their marriage, but she has grown to love him and refuses. When he is released, they resume their marriage and become godparents to McCoy's son.

Film Entries, 1911-1920.

William A. Howell standing front center.
(Photo from collection of Myra Van Haden).

Thanhouser Film Corporation
1915 - 1916.

I discovered an early website about the Thanhouser Films and wrote Ned Thanhouser. We exchanged information and photos related to my grandfather. After sending him several photos, Ned sent me a CD of the history of Thanhouser Films in 1997.

Biographical Notes: William A. Howell was born in Cleveland, Ohio in 1877, and was educated at Fordham University, Bronx, New York. His stage career included playing in The Thief, New Dominion, Experience, and other productions. He directed stock companies in Baltimore, Cleveland, Cincinnati, and Rochester. For Poli's New England theatres, he was a director of and actor in melodramas. His screen career included Rex, Universal, Majestic, Gene Gauntier Co., and C. C. Field, in such films as False Evidence, Scrap of Paper, All Rivers Meet at the Sea, The Boosters, and others.

He was hired by Edwin Thanhouser in the summer of 1915 and reported for work on Tuesday morning, August 27th. For the Thanhouser Film Corporation he was involved in the Falstaff Department, directing and acting in comedies. During the first several months of 1916 he was directing at Thanhouser's Jacksonville studio. William A. Howell directed the May 1916 Arrow release of The Tight Rein. In autumn 1916 a directory listing noted he was 6' tall, weighed 185 pounds, and had brown hair and gray eyes. His pastimes included horseback riding, swimming, painting, writing, and motoring. He lived at 2850 Concourse, Fordham, New York, and was represented in 1916 by the Amalgamated Photoplay Company, 220 West 42nd Street, New York City.

Note: In several notices his surname appeared as "Howard."

"Thanhouser Films: An Encyclopedia and History 1909 to 1918"
by Q. David Bowers, Copyright©1997.

Myra V. Howell, William's widow had written "Directing Motion Pictures in the 1910s in New York and Florida" on the bottom of this photograph. Directing assistant, scriptman, Lloyd F. Lonergan, and William A. Howell. (Photo from the collection of Myra Van Haden).

Thanhouser Film Corporation

Early in 1915, Edward Thanhouser returned to take over the Thanhouser Film Corporation and brought about many changes. Edwin Thanhouser hired William A. Howell in the summer on 1915 and he reported to work on Friday morning, August 27th. At Thanhouser he was involved in the Falstaff Department, directing and acting in comedies.

THANHOUSER ANNOUNCEMENT.

Beginning with Monday and every Monday thereafter Falstaff comedies will be released at the rate of two single-reelers weekly instead of one, as heretofore. This announcement means much at this time, when comedy is conceded the most difficult branch of the production.

When Edwin Thanhouser launched the Falstaff comedy brand it was with a very definite policy in view. This was to build a consistent, reliable product of the kind of comedy that will not wear out. That he has succeeded in this is proved when the market demands the doubling of the output.

The New Rochelle Pioneer, Saturday,
August 14, 1915.

INCREASES HIS OUTPUT AGAIN

Thanhouser Will Release a Three-Reel Production Every Third Week for Mutual.
NINE DIRECTORS WORKING

The newly arranged Mutual schedule outputs in the country.

There are now the following directors at work-Platt, Moore, Sullivan, Ellery, Ward, Mitchell, Clarendon, Howell, and Mayo. Another director will be engaged, making 10 in all. Three of these are comedy directors who have made good and are now producing only for the Falstaff comedy brand, two of which are released weekly. The operation of 10 companies has necessitated a corresponding enlargement of the staff.

The Morning Telegraph, Motion Picture Weekly,
Sunday, August 15, 1915.

October 1915 saw the release of a string of rhythmically-named Falstaff comedies on Mondays and Thursdays. Cousin Clara's Cook Book, issued on October 4th, received an enthusiastic review from The Moving Picture World.

Thanhouser's November releases began on the first day of the month with the one-reel Falstaff comedy, Freddie, the Fake Fisherman. By now the alliterative titles were standard with Falstaff films, as the list of the month's other Falstaff pictures demonstrates: "Clarissa's" Charming Calf, Lulu's Lost Lotharios, The Film Favorite's Finish, Hannah's Hen-Pecked Husband, A Cunning Canal-Boat Cupid, The Postmaster of Pineapple Plains, The Villainous Vegetable Vender, and Foiling Father's Foes. With the exception of The Moving Picture World, trade journals declined to review the comedies.

Thanhouser Film Corporation

Finest Movie Studio in the South to Open in December

Thanhouser Film Corporation's Studio on East Eighth Street Will Be Ready for Occupancy Within a Month—Will Have a Payroll of $1,000 Per Day—Many Stars Will Be Here at Different Times It Is Stated.

Following preliminary work which has been accomplished already, announcement was made yesterday that the finest motion picture studio in the South at least will be that of the Thanhouser Film Corporation at Eighth Street, just east of Main Street.

The plant will be ready by early December, and at that time some of the world's greatest stars will be in Jacksonville to act before the cameras of that concern. An expenditure of $25,000 or more is being made in renewing the building of the old Rico Laundry property which has been secured.

It is stated that when the producing season opens there will be a payroll of upwards of $1,000 per day. Parts if not, this season. In a visit here of Robert Holpen, chief carpenter, with Alfred H. Moses, technical expert of the corporation, some days ago expressed themselves as well pleased with the chances offered.

Over a month ago Edwin Thanhouser, president of the company, paid a call to Jacksonville and looked over various sites. Mr. Thanhouser states that the climatic conditions here are ideal for a large number of important pictures which he has in the planning.

A payroll of seventy-five or so people will be the case here at all times with the studio, among the stars being Florence LaBudie, Gladys Helett, Mignon Anderson, Morris Foster, Harris Gordon, Boyd Marshall, Thomas Curine and Wayne Avery.

The Florida Times-Union, Friday,
November 5, 1915.

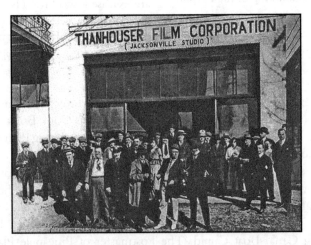

Thanhouser Studio, Jacksonville, about January 1916. (Photo courtesy of the American Museum of the Moving Image, Lawrence Williams Collection).

Thanhouser Film Corporation

Cousin Clara's Cook Book
Falstaff Arrow Film Corporation - 4 October 1915.
Released by Thanhouser Film Corporation
and Mutual Film Corporation.

Cast: **William A. Howell** as Bing's the Book Agent, **Winifred Lane** as Cousin Clara, **Riley Chamberlain** as Clara's Invalid Father.

COUSIN'S CLARA'S COOK BOOK (Falstaff), Oct. 4. - This pictures entertainingly the adventures of a book agent. At first unsuccessful, he pretends to be a maniac and thus obtains a pocketful of orders. The photography is very good and the situations contain considerable humor.

Moving Picture World, October 16, 1915, p. 440.

Unknown baseball player and William A. Howell. Photograph #192.4
(Photo from collection of Myra Van Haden).

Thanhouser Film Corporation

Freddie, The Fake Fisherman
Falstaff Arrow Film Corporation - 1 November 1915.
Released by Thanhouser Film Corporation
and Mutual Film Corporation.
Possibly directed by William A. Howell.

Cast: **William A. Howell** as Freddie, **Winifred Lane** as his Sweetheart, **George T. Welsh** as the Father.

FREDDY, THE FAKE FISHERMAN (Falstaff), Nov. 1. - In which a young man poses as an expert fisherman to please the girl's father. The fishing trip is quite a wild affair, with plenty of accidents in it. This is nicely pictured and amusing.

Moving Picture World, October 30a, 1915, p. 968.

Hannah's Henpecked Husband
Falstaff Arrow Film Corporation - 15 November 1915.
Released by Thanhouser Film Corporation
and Mutual Film Corporation.
Possibly directed by William A. Howell.

Cast: **Carey L. Hastings** as Hannah, **Boyd Marshall** as Henry, her husband, **William A. Howell** as Felix, her Admirer.

HANNAH'S HENPECKED HUSBAND (Falstaff), Nov. 15.- This is not an especially commendable comedy. It is a farcically-told story of a husband who was maltreated to a rather large extent and of a musician with whom the wife falls in love. Because the wife tells the musician that she cannot marry him because she is not free, he starts out to commit suicide and run across the husband contemplating the same thing. Finally they both decide that they had better continue to live.

Moving Picture World, November 13, 1915, p. 1312.

Thanhouser Film Corporation

The Optimistic Oriental Occults
Falstaff Arrow Film Corporation - 3 January 1916.
Released by Thanhouser Film Corporation
and Mutual Film Corporation.
Directed by William A. Howell.

Cast: **Riley Chamberlain** as August, the rich uncle, **Frances Keyes** as the postmistress, **Boyd Marshall** as first Nephew, **Frank Herbert** as second Nephew, Frank McNish as a Cousin, **Walter Hiers** as another Cousin.

THE OPTIMISTIC ORIENTAL OCCULTS (Falstaff), Jan. 3. - An amusing comedy of an exaggerated sort. Riley Chamberlain, a rich old fellow hates his relatives because they want his money. He contrives many schemes to keep them off his place. The substitution of the fake corse is a good feature. A pleasing comedy.

Moving Picture World, January 8, 1916, p. 262.

**Boyd Marshall and Riley Chamberlain as August,
the rich uncle. Photograph #192.2
(Photo from collection of Myra Van Haden).**

Thanhouser Film Corporation

George K. Hollister, a cameraman with Thanhouser from 1915 to 1916, had worked with Gene Gauntier when William Howell was also there. He was the cameraman with William Howell directing the Falstaff films for Thanhouser at Jacksonville, Florida until he accepted an offer from the C. C. Field Motion Picture Company of Miami in April 1916. This is the same time that his wife, Alice, and William A. Howell accepted an offer from C. C. Field.

When the C. C. Field Motion Picture Company folded, George Hollister went to New York City and was the cameraman for William A. Howell's short lived Gathem Films, Inc. during 1918.

**Possibly George K. Hollister who was the cameraman
on the following Falstaff films
with William A. Howell, the director of these Falstaff comedies.
(Photo from the collection of Myra Van Haden).**

Thanhouser Film Corporation

Scenes Of Action In The
Photo's Taken From Thanhouser Plant
"Perkins Peace Party.."

(Upper) Fatty Hires, Louise Bates, Violet Hite, Riley Chamberlain, (Lower)
W. A. Howell, Director, Billy Sullivan, Asst., Geo. Hollister, Cameraman
(Photo from The Sunday Times-Union, in the
collection of Terris C. Howard).

Some Interesting Side Lights on the Thanhouser Plant at Jacksonville, Revealed During a Personally Conducted Tour of the Buildings With W. Ray Johnston

That Jacksonville is destined to become the Mecca for the moving picture industry, is evident from the fact that within the past few months several important companies have established studios in this city, among them being the Thanhouser Company, which has established a permanent plant at 33 and 37 East Eighth Street, where they have fitted out one of the most up-to-date moving picture factories to be found anywhere in the South.

Having received a cordial invitation to inspect the Jacksonville studios of the Thanhouser Film Corporation, a representative...art of picture making.

Thanhouser Film Corporation

SCENES OF ACTION IN THE THANOUSER PLANT - Continued

Entering the enclosed stage, Director W. Eugene Moore and company and Director Leo Wirth were busy directing Harris Gordon in a big dramatic scene in a forthcoming Mutual Masterpicture to be known as "The Oval Diamond." Mr. Gordon will be remembered by Jacksonville fans who saw him playing the lead in "The Mill-on-the Floss," shown at the Prince Theatre last week. The Oval Diamond is to be a five-reel play.

On the opposite end of this large glass-covered stage, Director William A. Howell was at work on a one-reel Falstaff comedy entitled Perkins' Peace Party, and right here is where the Times-Union photographer got busy.... The picture features popular Louise Emerald Bates, better known as the Falstaff Girl, and funny Fatty (Walter) Hiers, who will remembered by the Jacksonville citizens as having been connected with the Majestic and Lubin companies in Jacksonville. From the appearance of Fatty, who was playing as a chef in the ship's galley as a hose was being plied on him by co-director Billy Sullivan, your scribe became of the opinion that playing in the movie comedies is not all joy, and that he did not care to become a Falstaff funmaker. The picture, which was started in New York, is now nearing completion, a large number of the scenes having been taken aboard the Clyde Line's Mohawk while the company was enroute from New York to Jacksonville.

At the side of the enclosed stage the newspaper men...was working on a five reeler, entitled 'What Doris Grey Did."

The Sunday Times-Union, Sunday,
January 16, 1916.

Snow, Storm and Sunshine
Falstaff Arrow Film Corporation - 10 February 1916.
Released by Thanhouser Film Corporation
and Mutual Film Corporation.
Directed by William A. Howell.
Cinematography by George K. Hollister.

Cast: **Riley Chamberlain** as the Constable, **Walter Hier** as the Tramp.

SNOW STORM AND SUNSHINE (Falstaff), Feb. 10. - A comedy number, relying more on pictorial effects than plot. Two tramps witness a young man taking a bath amid snow and ice. This is the best feature; it has been done before, but is astonishing and unusual. The contrasting scenes are taken in the South. A fairly strong novelty.

Moving Picture World, February 19, 1916, p. 1151.

Perkin's Peace Party

**Falstaff Arrow Film Corporation - 17 February 1916.
Released by Thanhouser Film Corporation
and Mutual Film Corporation.
Directed by William A. Howell.
Cinematography by George K. Hollister.**

Cast: **Walter Hier** as Henry Perkins, **Louise Bates** as Mrs. Perkins, **Riley Chamberlain** as the Sailor.

PERKIN'S PEACE PARTY (Falstaff), Feb. 24. - An unhappy professor, who cannot get along without quarreling with his wife, decides to go to Europe and stop the war. He and a friend start on a vessel, but are forced to scrub decks and do other hard labor. He returns to find his wife waiting with a horsewhip. The idea is a quietly amusing one and is quite pleasingly worked out.

Moving Picture World, March 4, 1916, p. 1494.

Thanhouser Film Corporation

During the first six months of 1916 William Howell was directing Falstaff comedies at Thanhouser's Jacksonville, Florida studio. This production company was known as the Falstaff Southern Company and was headed by Director William A. Howell with Louise Emerald Bates, Riley Chamberlain and Walter Hiers.

THANHOUSERS HERE
TO WORK AT STUDIO
ON 8TH STREET

Announcement Was Made Yesterday That Everything Will Be in Operation Within Two Weeks.

WILL BE MODERN PLANT;
THOROUGH IN EQUIPMENT

President Thanhouser Will Arrive in City Early Next Week to Look Over Branch.

The Thanhouser studio, just east of Main on Eighth street, will be as busy as a beehive within the course of a fortnight, according to the statement of George Grimmer, one of the officials of the corporation, on his arrival in the city yesterday. Next week Edwin Thanhouser, president of the company, and Lloyd Lonergan, chief of the scenario department, will arrive. The first work to be done will be five-reel features and one- and two-reel comedies, the latter of the famous Falstaff series.

A number of the actors and actresses, as well as cameramen and technical experts, arrived in the city yesterday aboard the Clyde steamer Mohawk. Mr. Grimmer and several of the officials made the trip here over the Seaboard Air Line Railway. Other workers, officials and artists will be reaching the city within the next few days.

Entirely Modern Plant.

The Thanhouser plant here on East Eighth Street will be one of the most complete in the country when it is finished in a few days. Two stages, one of a open-air sort and the other of the latest glass and steel construction, will be used. In the old Rico Laundry building, which was taken over by the studio, a great transformation has been wrought.

"I believe our people will have the most commodious dressing rooms in the country and everything arranged in convenient fashion," stated Mr. Grimmer.

Showing a most accurate knowledge of the minute details of film making, Mrs. Grimmer was the companion of her husband in a trip out to the studio yesterday afternoon. She states that all connected with the Thanhouser Corporation are looking forward to the sojourn here with pleasure.

Some Who Have Arrived.

Numerous members of the two companies who will first begin work here arrived yesterday and soon got comfortably located. They included Mr. and Mrs. Arthur Bauer, Mr. and Mrs. Harris Gordon, Eugene Moore, William Howell, Mr. Wirth, Mr. and Mrs. A. H. Moses and two children,

Miss Barbara Gilroy, Agnes Johnston, Miss V. Hite, Miss Palmer, and niece, Sully Guard, Leo Post, Billy Sullivan, Boyd Marshall, Riley Chamberlin, Frank Johns, with Messrs. Brokaw, Alexander and Christie.

The site of the studio here was personally selected by Edwin Thanhouser, president of the company, in a visit to Jacksonville several months ago. He was taken over the city and suburbs by George E. Leonard. After a consideration of many places he chose the Eighth street site. The plan of getting ready for actual production work had been hindered by the failure of necessary glass to arrive which is to be used in the covering of one of the studios.

The Florida Times-Union, Tuesday
December 21, 1915.

Thanhouser Film Corporation

THANHOUSER CO.
IN JACKSONVILLE
READY FOR WORK

Comedy and Dramatic
Companies Making
High Class Pictures in
Jacksonville - Other Companies
Coming Within Two Weeks.

The Thanhouser Motion Picture Company is now in Jacksonville ready for business at its modern plant on Eighth street, where it expects to work several companies during the winter season.

The comedy company is under the direction of William A. Howell, and the principal comedians are Riley Chamberlin, Walter Hiers and Louise Bates.

The dramatic company is under the direction of Eugene Moore, with the following players: Harris Gordon, Boyd Marshall, Barbara Gilroy, Sully Guard, India Palmer, George Post, Ray Johnston, Violet Hite, and Mabel Warren.

The technical director of the company is George Grimmer, and assistant directors are Leo Wirth and Billy Sullivan.

Mr. Alfred Moses, the photographic expert, has entire charge of the negative department.

Mr. Edwin Thanhouser and Lloyd Lonergan, scenario editor, will arrive today for a short stay in Jacksonville. In a few weeks two more dramatic companies will leave New Rochelle for Jacksonville.

Mr. Howell, comedy director, has been in Jacksonville before, as leading man of a stock company playing here years ago. Walter Hiers, fat boy comedian, has been here three winters, his engagements being with the Majestic and Lubin companies.

The Sunday Times-Union,
December 26, 1915.

Thanhouser Film Corporation

The year 1916 would prove to be one of great change for the Thanhouser Film Corporation. In January attention was focused on the Jacksonville studio, which had opened for production in late December with commencement of filming of The Oval Diamond. The warm climate and longer daylight hours permitted outdoor filming in Florida's tropical settings in the season when New Rochelle was cold and bleak. During the next several months there were many trade journal and newspaper articles devoted to Thanhouser's Southern activities.

Maud Muller Modernized
Falstaff Arrow Film Corporation - 2 March 1916.
Released by Thanhouser Film Corporation
and Mutual Film Corporation.
Directed by William A. Howell. Cinematography
by George K. Hollister.

Cast: **Louise Bates** as Maud Muller, **Riley Chamberlain** as the Judge.

MAUD MULLER MODERNIZED (Falstaff), March 2. - An entertaining parody on the Maud Muller poem, with poetical subtitles. She drives a Flivver, runs over the judge, and scares away his affections. A funny half reel of the nonsensical type.

Moving Picture World, March 11, 1916, p. 1666.

Thanhouser Film Corporation

One-reel Falstaff comedies, released each Tuesday and Thursday, commenced with A Clever Collie's Comeback on February 1ˢᵗ. In a film similar to the old Shep movies Lady played the part of the Thanhouser Collie. "The number will perhaps have special appeal to children," The Moving Picture World commented. Subsequent Falstaff comedies for the month of February 1916 included Harry's Happy Honeymoon, Booming the Boxing Business, Snow Storm and Sunshine, Perkins' Peace Party, Ruth's Remarkable Reception, and Rustie Reggie's Record. Few reviewers noticed the films.

Thanhouserites to Florida

Many Players and Directors Form Big Caravan from New Rochelle to Jacksonville.

Last week witnessed an exodus at the Thanhouser studios in New Rochelle. The big new home in Jacksonville was pronounced finished and three full companies were shipped off. The directors in charge are George Foster Platt, Eugene Moore and William Howell. These companies include fifty-five persons, which makes the Thanhouser initial delegation the largest that ever descended on Jacksonville. And more are to go.

Mr. Howell heads the Falstaff Comedy southern company, and Riley Chamberlin will be his chief comedian. Louise Emerald Bates, the blonde beauty, will play the female leads, and Mr. Howell also took with him Walter Hiers, the fat knockabout with the moon face. Boyd Marshall, the popular juvenile, will be seen in comedy straights.

The Thanhouser players will be housed in a beautiful studio which has been put up at an expense of $30,000. It is a permanent edifice with one of the largest glass roofs ever constructed. George Grimmer is in charge.

The Moving Picture World, January 15, 1916

William A. Howell, the Thanhouser-Falstaff director, has finished two pictures during the week. The first, Ambitious Awkward Andy, featuring Fatty Hiers and Riley Chamberlin; and the other, Maud Muller Modernized, featuring the popular Louise Emerald Bates, better known as the Falstaff Girl. Mr. Howell's next subject will be Theodore's Terrible Thirst, with an all-star comedy cast including Riley Chamberlin, Walter Hiers, Louise Emerald Bates and Violet Hite.

The Sunday Times-Union,
Sunday, January 23, 1916.

Ambitious Awkward Andy
**Falstaff Arrow Film Corporation - 9 March 1916.
Released by Thanhouser Film Corporation
and Mutual Film Corporation.
Directed by William A. Howell. Cinematography
by George K. Hollister.**

Cast: **Walter Hiers** as Andy, **Riley Chamberlain** as his Boss.

AMBITIOUS AWKWARD ANDY (Falstaff), March 9. - This, a clean amusing comedy, in which Andy, a colored office attendant, ambitious to better his position, tries all sorts of vocations with usually disastrous effects. His last offense before returning to his former job, is the accidental exploding of several types of dynamite. Very funny.

Moving Picture World, March 18, 1916, p. 1854.

Thanhouser Film Corporation

PERSONNEL OF THE TANHOUSER FILM CORPORATION NOW
PRODUCING THEIR FAMOUS PICTURES AT THEIR JAX STUDIO

Wm. A. Howell

(Photo from the collection of Myra Van Haden).

THANHOUSER FILM STUDIO HERE IS NOW COMPLETED

The studio of the Thanhouser Film Corporation, which has been under construction for several months is now completed and represents an expenditure of $50,000.

The city of Jacksonville is to be congratulated...who was photographing the scene.

The representative was also introduced to William A. Howell, director of the No. 1 company of the Thanhouser-Falstaff brand. He was directing a scene from "Perkins' Peace Party," featuring Louise Emerald Bates, the Falstaff girl, and Walter Hires, the Thanhouser fat boy. Fatty at this time was playing a chef on board the liner Mohawk, of the Clyde Lines, where the scene had been previously taken while the company was en route from New York to Jacksonville. Billy Sullivan, co-director of the Howell Company, was taking considerable delight in playing a hose of icy water on the chef and "Fatty" "registered" an expression of anything but pleasure. George. K. Hollister, formerly with Kalem's local company, was taking the picture.

The reporter was also shown through the company's property rooms....make your four Thanhouser companies located in this city, where several thousand dollars are being expended weekly for the movies.

The Sunday Metropolis,
January 23, 1916.

Thanhouser Film Corporation

HOWELL'S PRAYER WAS ANSWERED, IT HAS RAINED

Comedy Director for Thanhouser Company Gives an Interesting Interview.

Declaring that he has been constantly on his knees for weeks praying for a little rain so as to be able to take a needed rest, William A. Howell, comedy director for the Thanhouser Jacksonville company, entered the Hotel Mason Sunday with smiling face and proceeded to bore a poor newspaper reporter to death.

He was only asked for a few spare moments of his valuable time and here is the exact way he gave it:

"Yes, today I think I can spare you a few minutes, seeing it is all clouded up. You see, you have such confounded fine weather here that despite my prayer for rain I have been obliged to be at it every day since my arrival three weeks ago.

We took pictures on the boat coming from New York, set up our camera upon landing and have continued that tempo ever since. Tempo, as you know, is the prime factor in comedy. We move fast. The day of the slow, padded, three or more reels of comedy is doomed. A story told quickly and humorously in one reel is the only entertainment that I contribute to the vast program of the Thanhouser branch. I have here everything to bring these comedies to successful completion-Intelligent scenarios, excellent photography, talented comedians, perfect studios, both artificially lighted and open-air, all these, coupled with your glorious sunshine, cooperation of your civic body, business men, and householders, certainly make my work a pleasure.

ENTHUSED OVER JACKSONVILLE.

"Then, I ask you, why shouldn't I enthuse? In fact, since coming to Jacksonville I have taken a new interest in my work. There is no greater restraint to bubbling humor than to have to wait two or three days for fair weather conditions, such as they experience in New York at the present moment.

Your enthusiasm dies, so to speak, when you look out upon a bleak world; you may look funny to the other fellow, but believe me, you can't possibly see a joke when soaked to the skin with a promise of a fine touch of pneumonia.

Yes, I know, I have prayed for rain while here, but that was only to allow me to catch up with a couple of hours extra sleep and to get my scenarios in order. Scenarios? Yes, indeed, I have quite a collection - some finished but untrimmed - others in the making, and today I have received the first batch of comedy scenarios written around locations of Jacksonville and environs.

"How do I know that my scenarios match up with my locations? Well, that isn't so difficult. Immediately I read an accepted scenario, I have in my mind's eye the location for such a scene. If I am at a loss, there is my photographer to help me in my dilemma. And speaking of photographers I am somewhat more fortunate than some of my confreres, having at my service one George Hollister, a cameraman who has photographed almost everything photographic, in and around your city for the past six years, and if he is as good a weather prophet as he is a photographer, there will be no rest for the weary; according to his forecast, there is continuous fine weather for picture taking in Jacksonville nine months of the year. Help!"

The Sunday Metropolis, January 23, 1916.

Thanhouser Film Corporation

In March the twice-a-week Falstaff comedies began with Maud Muller Modernized, a satire on John Greenleaf Whittier's 19th century poem in which he told of a sweet country maiden who becomes enamored of a respected judge who stops by her farm to water his horse. The attraction is mutual, and as the man of law rides away he wistfully contemplates Maud's beauty and charm. As her memory lingers he realizes that his world of society and wealth is too different from hers to be reconciled. He weds a lady of fashion and power, and Maud takes a poor, unlearned man for a husband. As the years go by, Maud and the judge separately contemplate: "For of all sad words of tongue or pen, the saddest are these: 'It might have been.'" In the Falstaff parody Maud drives a car, runs over the judge, and frightens him away. Split at the end of the reel was a filler, Jungle Life in South America, which pictured venomous reptiles and various small mammals.

The quaintest novelty that has yet hit the moving picture industry is the way the titles of the Thanhouser Falstaff comedies alliterate. If anything could give them the face value of comedies, their titles do that trick. Here are a few of them, which were produced under the direction of William A. Howell, the Falstaff director now in Jacksonville: Cousin Clara's Cookbook, Bing-Bang Brothers, The Soap Suds Star, Snowstorm and Sunshine, Perkins' Peace Party, Ambitious Awkward Andy, Maud Muller Modernized, and Theodore's Terrible Thirst.

The Sunday Times-Union, Sunday, January 30, 1916.

Poster courtesy of "Thanhouser Films: An Encyclopedia and History" by Q. David Bowers, Thanhouser Company Film Preservation, Inc. Copyright©1997.

Thanhouser Film Corporation

THANHOUSER TOPICS

"Auto Edition"

After reading the Thanhouser Topics for the week we were tempted to change the heading to "Automobile Edition of Thanhouser Topics." These Thanhouser boys seem to be joy riders.

★ ★ ★

William McNulty had purchased a Flanders Runabout, latest model. Mac's lead evidently started a run on cars, for a number of other additions to the auto colony were reported soon after.

★ ★ ★

Alfred H. Moses, Jr., chief photographer and technical expert of the Thanhouser studios, is the owner of a new Saxon six. He motored to St. Augustine last Sunday to give it a tryout.

★ ★ ★

It is rumored that George A. Grimmer, manager of the Thanhouser Studio, has became the owner of a 90 horse power eight-cylinder Stutz. Mr. Grimmer could not be located up to time of going to press to confirm the report.

★ ★ ★

The Thanhouser studio purchased a Hup 20 Roadster last Thursday, which Mr. Platt made quick work of on Friday by sinking in the quicksand below Pablo Beach.

★ ★ ★

Riley Chamberlin continues to roll merrily along in his Ford five-passenger and says "It's the only way to travel."

★ ★ ★

Ethel Jewett, one of the heavy woman of the Thanhouser Company, made a trip along Atlantic Beach Sunday, via auto, and from the enthusiasm she displayed over the trip we are inclined to think that Miss Jewett's Overland will be coming down to Jacksonville on one of the early boats. It will be remembered that Miss Jewett won her car in a contest conducted last December by the Sunday Telegraph, New York City, when Miss Jewett was the second most popular motion picture actress, being led only by Clara Kimball Young, who received a seven-passenger car.

★ ★ ★

Billy Sullivan, an assistant director, at the Thanhouser plant, is the possessor of a new Reo roadster.

★ ★ ★

The latest recruit to the "Thanhouser Auto Club" is Wm. A. Howell, with a Marmon six-cylinder roadster purchased during the week.

★ ★ ★

And still they come. Frank Jobes has traded in his old car on a new Saxon Six.

★ ★ ★

Arthur Bauer, the popular heavy of the Thanhouser Company has taken a ride in every demonstration car in Jacksonville, but we don't see him driving his own car yet. Arthur will have seen all of Jacksonville surroundings if he don't buy soon.

★ ★ ★

Louise Emerald Bates may be seen any day making the trip from the

Seminole Hotel to the Eighth street studio in her National roadster. Some class to that car, Louise!

★ ★ ★

Violet Hite, a popular Thanhouser player, had the misfortune to sprain her ankle when she made a misstep in alighting from her automobile Sunday last. The sprain is mending nicely, under the doctor's care, and her smiling countenance is expected in the studio next week.

★ ★ ★

Boyd Marshall, the popular Thanhouser star is being featured in "The Hidden Valley." In the story Boyd is the son of an importer and is sent to South Africa as a special envoy by his father to look up the reason why the exportation from that country is so small. From that point the picture deals with his experiences in South Africa. Mr. Marshall will have excellent support in Mlle. Valkyrien, Les Post, Arthur Bauer and Frank Pariani. Those listed above are the only white people in the cast. The picture is being produced by Ernest Warde.

★ ★ ★

Director William A. Howell is working on a new Falstaff, entitled "Ruining Randall's Reputation," featuring Riley Chamberlain, supported by Walter Hires, Gladys Dore and Virginia Lee.

The Sunday Metropolis,
February 20, 1916.

Thanhouser Film Corporation

Big Increase in Mutual's Producing Forces

Corporation's business assumes such proportions that additional activities are needed to meet demand

A STATEMENT issuing from the home office of the Mutual Film Corporation announces a large increase in the acting forces and in the production activities of the American, Thanhouser, Horsley, Gaumont and Signal and Vogue film Companies, the picture output of which is released through Mutual exchanges.

To supplement the companies already at work on Mutual Masterpieces, De Luxe Edition, the American Film Corporation has organized another company with Winnifred Greenwood and Franklin Ritchie at the head. Miss Greenwood has been associated with the American for several years, appearing for the greater part of the time as the leading woman with Edward Coxen in the "Flying A' drama. Mr. Ritchie is one of the best known leading men of the picture profession, having been connected with Biograph and a number of Klaw and Erlanger productions. As a legitimate actor he is equally known, having been under the Frohman management for four years and the Belasco management for two years. He left the Biograph company to become a leading man for the American Film Company.

Four Thanhouser Directors At Work In Jacksonville, Fla.

There are four directors at work at the Jacksonville, Florida studios of the Thanhouser Company. The most recent addition to the players is Marion Swayne, the charming little ingénue who was last year the leading woman of the Gaumont Company. Among the others are Valkyrien (the Baroness DeWitz), who is starred in The Valkyrie and in the recent three-reel feature, The Cruise of Fate. Boyd Marshall, Thomas A. Curran, and Bert Delaney are among the players of drama, and Louise Emerald Bates, Riley Chamberlin, and Walter Hiers are comedy artists who are in Jacksonville.

The four directors are Ernest Warde, W. Eugene Moore, George Foster Platt, Mutual Masterpicture and three-reel feature directors, and William A. Howard, a "Falstaff" comedy director of long experience in motion pictures.

At the New Rochelle studio of the Thanhouser company Director Frederick Sullivan is producing Mister Shakespeare, Strolling Player, which will be full of spirit of Merry Englande and the Bard of Avon. Florence LaBadie is appearing in this production.

J. H. Gilmour, the well-known artist, who has recently been added to the Thanhouser forces; Robert Whittier, who made his first appearance in Mutual releases in Betrayed; John Lehmberg, Frank E. McNish and George Marlo are among the actors at the New Rochelle studios.

Reel Life, The Mutual Film Magazine, March 18, 1916.

The writer of the above article may have previously known William A. Howard or the Thanhouser studio released the information using the name William A. Howard instead of William A. Howell.

Thanhouser Film Corporation

Falstaff Comedies Force Market

Thanhouser Says Novelty Replaces Violence Profitably – Subjects Have Good Demand.

It is now about a year since Edwin Thanhouser launched one of his new ideas in the form of the Falstaff brand of comedy. It was at that time announced that these single reelers would represent the direct line of legitimate comedies in vogue. It was pointed out by Mr. Thanhouser that attention would be given first to story; that was the most conspicuous missing element of rapid-fire funny films. The genius of Lloyd Lonergan...was put into play, also Phil Lonergan, his able younger brother.

From the very first Note the big feature of the Falstaff brand was the oddity of the alliterative title; and they quickly caught on. The character of the subject is quickly proclaimed by such titles as "Perplexing Pickle Puzzle," "Busted But Benevolent," "Oscar the Oyster Opener," "Pedro the Punk Poet," "Pansy's Prison Pies," "Film Favorite's Finish," "Clarissa's Charming Calf," and others, all of them funny to the tongue and the ear. They caught on quickly and after a few releases the trade realized that Falstaffs were a different kind of comedy.

Then when the Mutual Exchanges were booking them out at a top rate, the "Wizard of New Rochelle" let fly his heavy artillery. He signed up Riley Chamberlin to appear in Falstaffs exclusively, and soon after that Louise Emerald Bates as well, the blonde Ziegfeld beauty who is now known as the Falstaff Girl. Claude Cooper, funmaster, was made an acting director, and Walter Hiers, the fat comedian, was engaged to foil Chamberlin. Claude Cooper then reached out for a fun partner and finally landed Frank E. McNish, the famous old eccentric comedian. While all of this was being done the Falstaff output was doubled to two a week, and William A. Howell was added to the directing staff.

The original Falstaff director was Arthur Ellery, and his company remained in New Rochelle when it came time to go to Florida. Ellery's grasp of legitimate comedy values makes him easily the most consistent performer in his line, and he gets his results through his very seriousness when he stages the funniest scenes. Frances Keyes is his chief comedy character, and her versatility will be amply exhibited in a forthcoming release entitled "Pansy Post, Protean, Player." Ellery's methods seem to assure positive results, possibly due to his success as a writer of comic short stories.

Under the present release schedule the two Falstaffs per week have established their following, but it is expected that new additions will be made to the staff which will put them over with still more vim and smash.

The Moving Picture World, April 15, 1916.

Left on Trip for Health Reasons

William A. Howell, director for the Falstaff Company at the Thanhouser studio, left Sunday morning on an automobile trip down the East Coast, where he expects to spend several weeks. Mr. Howell has been in bad health for several weeks and is making this trip a vacation.

The Florida Metropolis, Friday, March 31, 1916.

Thanhouser Film Corporation

The Falstaff schedule continued in March with *Oscar the Oyster Opener*, followed by *Ambitious Awkward Andy, Theodores's Terrible Thirst, Rupert's Rube Relation, Pansy Poet Protean Player, Pedro the punk Poet, Paul's Political Pull*, and *The Snow Shoveler's Sweetheart*, most of which were filmed in Jacksonville.

One-reel Falstaff films released in April included *Ruining Randall's Reputation, The Professor's Peculiar Precautions, Sapville's Stalwart Son, The Overworked Oversea Overseer, The Sailor's Smiling Spirit, Simple Simon's Schooling, Dad's Darling Daughters*, and *Willing Wendy to Willie*. By this time the release days of Falstaff films had been changed to Monday and Saturday. The few reviews that appeared in print were mostly favorable. During this period only the five-reel Mutual Masterpictures, DeLuxe Edition received widespread reviews. Thanhouser films of lesser length were ignored by the majority of film critics.

In the meantime the June schedule saw various Thanhouser films released on the Mutual program. The month began with a Falstaff release on Monday, the 1ˢᵗ, *The Dashing Druggist's Dilemma*, followed on Thursdays and Mondays by other one-reel comedies, including *The Skilful Sleigher's Strategy, The Kiddies' Kaptain Kidd, Freddie's Frigid Finish*, then a film which began a departure from alliteration: *Deteckters*. Then followed *Steven's Sweet Sisters, Politickers, Sammy's Semi-Suicide*, and *Disguisers*. The comedies with non-alliterative titles featured Claude Cooper as Oscar and Frank McNish as Conrad, in a team billed as the Oscar and Conrad Company.

In early June the Thanhouser Film Corporation released its final pictures on the Mutual program. *Other People's Money*, a five-reel Mutual Masterpicture, DeLuxe Edition, was issued on the 1ˢᵗ and starred Gladys Hulette. Reviews were mixed. *Peterson's Pitiful Plight*, a Falstaff film, was released on the 3ʳᵈ, followed by another Falstaff comedy, *Advertisementers*, on the 5ᵗʰ. Then came *John Brewster's Wife* in two reels on the 6ᵗʰ, followed by two Falstaff comedies, *Where Wives Win* on the 10ᵗʰ and *Real Estaters* on the 12ᵗʰ. *Brothers Equal*, a two-reel drama issued on the 13ᵗʰ, was followed by *The Window of Dreams* in three reels on the 15ᵗʰ. The scenario, by Agnes Christine Johnson, a prolific writer on the Thanhouser staff, featured those old traditional cast names, Jack and May, the latter played by Grace DeCarlton. *Doughnuts*, a Falstaff comedy issued on the 17ᵗʰ, completed the releases for the month.

Thanhouser Film Corporation

Theodore's Terrible Thirst
Falstaff Arrow Film Corporation - 14 March 1916.
Released by Thanhouser Film Corporation
and Mutual Film Corporation.
Directed by William A. Howell. Cinematography
by George K. Hollister.

Cast: **Riley Chamberlain** as Theodore, **Frank McNeish** as Theodore's Son, **Louise Bates**.

THEODORE'S TERRIBLE THIRST (Falstaff), March 14. - A comedy number, containing some good humor of the quiet sort. The son places his father on a desert island to make him stop drinking, so they [can] obtain the inheritance money. The scheme works in spite of the father's protests. This will get a number of smiles.

Moving Picture World, March 25, 1916, p. 2031.

Rupert's Rube Relation
Falstaff Arrow Film Corporation - 16 March 1916.
Released by Thanhouser Film Corporation
and Mutual Film Corporation.
Directed by William A. Howell.
Cinematography by George K. Hollister.

Cast: **Riley Chamberlain** as Theodore, **Walter Hiers** as Rupert, **Frank McNeish** as a Relative,

RUPERT'S RUBE RELATION (Falstaff), March 16. - An interesting farce comedy in which Uncle Josh, the uncle of Rupert, known as the Rural Bohemian among his city associates, is lured to town and surprises the boys by his insusceptibility to shock when taken to a cabaret performance. Uncle Josh proves himself to be quite equal to the occasion. A very amusing farce.

Moving Picture World, March 25, p. 2031.

Paul's Political Pull
Falstaff Arrow Film Corporation - 28 March 1916.
Released by Thanhouser Film Corporation
and Mutual Film Corporation.
Directed by William A. Howell.
Cinematography by George K. Hollister.

Cast: **Walter Hiers** as Paul Jasper, **Riley Chamberlain** as Sport Costigan.

PAUL'S POLITICAL PULL (Falstaff), March 28. - A comedy number, in which two brothers impose upon their fat younger brother. The latter endures their cruel treatment, but when the uncle says he will leave his money to the one who does the most work, he contrives to win the prize. The humor is of a quiet sort and proves quite entertaining.

Moving Picture World, April 1, 1916, p. 106.

Thanhouser Film Corporation

Ruining Randall's Reputation
Falstaff Arrow Film Corporation - 3 April 1916.
Released by Thanhouser Film Corporation
and Mutual Film Corporation.
Directed by William A. Howell.
Cinematography by George K. Hollister.

Cast: **Riley Chamberlain** as Rivington Randall, **Gladys Dore** as his Niece, **Walter Hiers** as the Niece's Suitor.

RUINING RANDALL'S REPUTATION (Falstaff), April 3. - Riley Chamberlain appears in this as a guardian uncle who refused to let his niece wed. His enemies run him for congress and proceed to put up all manner of political tricks on him. He is glad to step out and withdraws his opposition to the love affair. This has a number of quite amusing situations in it.

Moving Picture World, April 15, 1916, p. 463.

The Professor's Peculiar Precautions
Falstaff Arrow Film Corporation - 8 April 1916.
Released by Thanhouser Film Corporation
and Mutual Film Corporation.
Directed by William A. Howell.
Cinematography by George K. Hollister.

Cast: **Riley Chamberlain** as The Professor's Rival, **Joseph Phillips** as Professor Pert, **Winifred Lane** as The Girl.

THE PROFESSOR'S PECULIAR PRECAUTIONS (Falstaff), April 8. - An amusing comedy in which two rival professors of mineralogy figure. The poverty stricken professor is obliged to sell a valuable diamond to his rival who demonstrates to him at the same time the burglar-proof devices with which his wonderful samples are protected. Too frequent use of these devices without reason provoke the police, fire departments, etc., to the extent that when a real alarm call is sent in from his source no notice is taken of it. This fact, of course occasions some queer situations.

Moving Picture World, April 15, 1916, p. 463.

The Sailor's Smiling Spirit
Falstaff Arrow Film Corporation - 17 April 1916.
Released by Thanhouser Film Corporation
and Mutual Film Corporation.
Directed by William A. Howell.
Cinematography by George K. Hollister.

Cast: **Walter 'Fatty; Hiers** at The Smiling Sailor, **Gladys Dore** as his Wife, **Riley Chamberlain** as the Wealthy Greengrocer.

THE SAILOR'S SMILING SPIRIT (Falstaff), April 17. - Riley Chamberlain and Fatty Hiers appear in this amusing comedy. The former is a grocer who covets the latter's wife. He places bombs in the sailor's vessel, but the latter turns up unexpectedly after his supposed death. This is a quietly amusing subject. The homecoming is a good scene.

Moving Picture World, April 22, 1916, p. 647.

Thanhouser Film Corporation

Dad's Darling Daughters

Falstaff Arrow Film Corporation - 24 April 1916.
Released by Thanhouser Film Corporation
and Mutual Film Corporation.
Directed by William A. Howell.
Cinematography by George K. Hollister.

Cast: **Riley Chamberlain** as Dad, **Violet Hiet** as his Daughter, **Walter Hiers** as the Daughter's Suitor.

DAD'S DARLING DAUGHTERS (Falstaff), April 24. - Riley Chamberlain is featured in this as the father of five girls. He sets their lovers to sawing wood, while he sits on the porch. After they are married the various sons-in-law get even by making the old man work when he visits them. The plot is nonsensical, but contains a good idea of the quietly amusing sort.

Moving Picture World, May 6, 1916, p. 989.

The Kiddies' Kaptain Kidd

Falstaff Arrow Film Corporation - 8 May 1916.
Released by Thanhouser Film Corporation
and Mutual Film Corporation.
Directed by William A. Howell.
Cinematography by George K. Hollister.

Cast: **Riley Chamberlain** as the rich Uncle, **Walter Hiers** as his Son, **Louise Emeral Bates** as the Stenographer.

CAPTAIN KIDD (Falstaff), May 8. - Riley Chamberlain's impersonation of the uncles who generously signed over his millions to an ungrateful nephew and went to live on a house boat, is pleasing. The nephew fails to provide for the wants of the generous relative who becomes obliged to dig oysters for a living. A young woman sees him digging up a box out of the sand, visits him and learns the situation, and finally starts a report that the old man has dug a Captain Kidd's treasure for the sea beach. Some children figure in the story believing him to be the real Captain Kidd. The nephew gets taken in on the treasure box, for after returning to his uncle what he has given him in anticipation of more personal gain, he finds that the box contains only rotten oysters.

Moving Picture World, May 13, 1916, p. 1182.

Sammy's Semi-Suicide
Falstaff Arrow Film Corporation - 27 May 1916.
Released by Thanhouser Film Corporation
and Mutual Film Corporation.
Directed by William A. Howell.

Cast: **Walter Hiers** as Sammy, **Frances Keyes** as his Sweetheart.

SAMMY'S SEMI-SUICIDE (Falstaff), May 27. - An amusing office comedy, featuring the corpulent Walter Hiers as a young man in love. He threatens suicide when things do not go right, and makes one or two unsuccessful efforts in that direction. In spite of the grimness of the subject this is treated in good burlesque style and is quite successful.

Moving Picture World, June 3, 1916, p. 1713.

Thanhouser Film Corporation

Doughnuts
**Falstaff Arrow Film Corporation - 17 June 1916.
Released by Thanhouser Film Corporation
and Mutual Film Corporation.
Directed by William A. Howell.**

Cast: **Riley Chamberlain** as the Conductor, **Gladys Leslie** as his Wife, **Frances Keyes** as his Mother, **Walter Hiers** as the Thief.

The filming commenced sometime in late March or early April 1916.

DOUGHNUTS (Falstaff), June 17. - Riley Chamberlain appears in this as a street car conductor on a vacation. He marries a girl who cannot cook, and her food brings him weird nightmares. The dog and the fat boy eat her doughnuts and both are sent to the hospital. A light comedy subject with smiles running all through it.

Moving Picture World, June 24, 1916, p. 2262.

William A. Howell directing Motion Pictures in Florida or Hollywood. Leading lady, assistant, writer, secretary, and William A. Howell. (Photo from the collection of Myra Van Haden).

Arrow Film Corporation

The Tight Rein
Arrow Film Corporation - 15 May 1916.
Released by Pathé
Produced by Howell Hansel and Directed
by William A. Howell.

SERIAL FILMS

"THE TIGHT REIN"

The Second Two-Part Episode of the Serial, "Who's Guilty," Produced by the Arrow Film Corporation, and Featuring Tom Moore and Anna Nilsson. Released by Pathe, May 15.

Jack McCall, a wealthy
man's son .... Tom Moore

Amy Prentice,
a mill-worker .... Anna Nilsson

Jeremiah McCall,
Jack's father .... Arthur Donaldson

Mathew Jordan,
business rival .... George Dupre

Gertrude Jordan, his
daughter .... Mildred Havens

Richard Babson, dept
store owner .... J. Albert Hall

The "Who's Guilty" series will fill a popular demand for photodramas of the type, for each week's release will be an individual drama, having no dependency upon a preceding feature, nor any connection with the release that follows. It is to be hoped that the forthcoming releases of the series will be kept up to the standard set by the first two.

"The Tight Rein" as a two-reeler is excellent and equal in interest and dramatic values to many a five reel feature. It is based upon a strong theme, through perhaps an old one, and is buoyed up by the meritorious acting of Miss Nilsson and Mr. Moore. Mr. Lawrence McGill's careful preparation of the picture is apparent throughout. Anna Nilsson's interpretation of Mrs. Wilson Woodrow's character of a factory girl is highly commendable. Tom Moore, natural and with his mind on the subject, is well chosen. The rest of the cast lends able support.

Through working in the silk mills of his wealthy father, Jack McCall is kept upon a meagre allowance, not even given the salary of a factory hand. And yet, the elder McCall is ambitious for his son, for when Jack's attentions to a factory girl, Amy, are discovered, the girl is "black-listed" and discharged, and Jack is put under his father's surveillance. In the motion picture world the road chosen by such girls is too frequently the one that leads down, not up, the hill. Amy, in New York, becomes the victim of Babson, a department store owner, to whom she has applied for work. She is no longer the poor, hard working girl in tattered dresses and lunch pail on arm. A transformation has taken place, and when Jack appropriates five hundred of his father's money he thinks due him, and after a long search in new York, finds Amy, she is in the guise of a lady of leisure. They meet in a restaurant, and she with Babson attempts to escape Jack's recognition, for fear that he would read the truth. He goes up to the gaudy Amy but she will not recognize him, on the plea that there has been some mistake. Then follows a fight between Jack and Babson, in which several tables are overturned and the diners thrown in a panic. They escape to Amy's apartments and while forgiving the past, with vows to live only for the future and each other, enter Babson. the store owner draws a revolver and aiming it at the cowering Amy, fires. In his attempt to take the weapon away from Babson, Jack also falls with a bullet in his heart. Placing the revolver in McCall's lifeless hand, Babson slinks from the room. The papers accuse Jack of the dual tragedy, and the grief-stricken father is horrified.

Upon whom should the guilt of the tragedy be placed? Perhaps the elder McCall; but that is a question which you must try to solve for yourself-"Who's Guilty?"

F. S.
The New York Dramatic Mirror,
Saturday, May 20, 1916.

Arrow Film Corporation

The Tight Rein

"Who's Guilty?" Series Ready

First Release Scheduled for May 8–Eight Installments Have Been Completed and Delivered-- Interesting Questions Portrayed.

IT IS NOW is certain that before May 8, the date of the release of the first photo-novel in Pathe's "Who's Guilty?" series, produced by Arrow Film Corporation, at least eight and probably nine of the fourteen photo-novels comprising this series will have been delivered by the producers to Pathe. This in itself marks a record in photo-play production even for a record-breaking series.

It has made possible the delivery by Pathe to the many newspapers which will run the "Who Guilty?" stories of six complete novels prior to the publication of the first one. Thereby the newspapers have enabled to give these stories unusually fine space and layouts.

It has been decided to release these pictures in the following sequences: "Puppets of Fate," on May 8; "The Tight Rein," on May 15; "The Tangled Web," on May 22; "The Silent Shame," on May 29; and "Sowing the Wind," on June 5. These are the first five of the "Who's Guilty?" series.

The Moving Picture World, May 13, 1916.

"Who's Guilty?"

First and Second of the Fourteen Two Part Episodes of the New Pathe Serial Based on Crime of Circumstance.
Reviewed by Margaret I. MacDonald.
"The Tight Rein."

"The Tight Rein," which, by the way, oversteps the first number In

excellence of story, has been produced by Howell Hansel for the Arrow Film Corporation. In this instance the victims of circumstances are the son of a wealthy mill owner and a pretty young girl who works in the mills. The son, played by Tom Moore, works in his father's office, is paid no regular salary, and is supplied very sparingly with money. At a later date his father's action in discharging the girl he loves so incenses him that he takes money from the safe and goes away to the city in search of her, leaving a note for his father which states what he has done. After knocking about the city squandering the money, he happens on the girl in a restaurant where she is in company with a man who has ruined her; a fight ensues, and he flees with the girl to her apartment, where they are followed by the man, who shoots the girl and himself. An accusation is of course brought against the mill owner's son for murder.

The stories of both numbers have been written by Mrs. Wilson Woodrow, and picturized by E. A. Bingham and Albert S. Levino.

The Moving Picture World, May 27, 1916.

Pathe Exchange, Inc.

WHO'S GUILTY? No. 2 "The Tight Rain" (Feature - 2 Parts - May 15). - This picture tells the story of two wealthy mill owners, one with a high-strung son and the other with a high-minded daughter-who wish to perpetuate the union of their factories through the mating of their children. Now the son of the one man respects the daughter of the other, but there his interest in her ceases; he loves one of his father's mill-hands, and she one of the minor employees in her father's place. When the son marries as his father wishes him to, he is to become a partner in the joint factories. The girl, however, has no escape from the deadly struggle for existence except marriage; and her ideals of marriage forbid this step for selfish purposes.

When the fathers discover that their plans are likely to be thwarted the girl not only is discharged but she Is black-listed in the town. Yet she and her mother are dependent solely on her meagre earnings. The son is tied even more closely to dependence on his father by having even his small allowance stopped. Here Is fertile ground for rebellion-and rebellion there is. The girl goes to a nearby city where she becomes one of many of a kind. The son searches for her, finds her, and is alone with her but a moment when the man she is dependent on rushes in, and misinterpreting their meeting, shoots both. Who's Guilty?

The Moving Picture World, May 27, 1916.

C. C. Motion Picture Company

The C. C. Field Motion Picture Company aka Field's Feature Films Company erected a fifteen thousand dollar concrete and tile studio on South Miami Avenue at 25th Street in Miami, Florida. Two companies of forty-four "actor and actresses, camera men, carpenters, property men, scenario men, electricians and every sort of expert need to manufacture feature films" arrived in April 1916. This studio was headed by Charles C. Field, who had been the president of the Prismatic Film Company in New York, and backed by Thomas J. Peters.

FLORIDA FILM FLASHES

Jacksonville, Fla. (Special).-Riley Chamberlain, of Thanhouser, has left for New Rochelle, but expects to return here in September.

The C. C. Field Motion Picture Company has completed their studio at Miami, and players from here who have accepted engagements with the company are: Alice Hollister, George K. Hollister, Howard Hall, and William A. Howell, formerly a director with Thanhouser.

E. O. Uedemann.

The New York Dramatic Mirror, Saturday, April 29, 1916.

FLORIDA FILM FLASHES

Jacksonville, Fla. (Special).-The C. C. Field Film Company's studio at Miami is expected to be completed this week. The company has been busy for some days and the following are in the cast: Howard Hall, Chap Field, Chester DeVonde, George Field, William Howell, Ruth Field, Kilbourne Gordon, Charles Graham, Richard Lile, Sidney Riggs, Jack Sears, Frank Tarbutte, Jack Reynolds, George Hollister, Carl Von Hoffman, Robert Minck, John Waglorn, Jesse Mitchell, A. Goodell, Ezra Walck, T. Regan, P. Hahn, Nora Barrey, Walter Miller, Maxine Brown, Alice Hollister, Irva Ross, Julia Calhoun, Marlon Wagion, Dora Dearborn, Jean Armour, Grace Gordon, Jose Vergilo, Charlotte Westervelt, Jessie Reed, Fay Lile, Mary Mitchell, Lizzie Brown, Viola Miller, Mrs. Ross, and Mr. and Mrs. C. C. Field.

E. O. Uedemann.

The New York Dramatic Mirror, Saturday, May 6, 1916.

Field Feature Film Company Studio on South Miami Avenue about August 1916. (Hoit photo from Miami Herald courtesy of the Florida State Archives).

Field's Feature Films Company

The Human Orchid
Fields Feature Films Company – June 1916.
Produced and Directed by Charles C. Fields.

Cast: **Irva Ross** as Ruth Brooks, **Charles Graham, Walter Miller, Julia Calhoun, Howard Hall, Noah Berry, Jean Armour,** and possibly **William A. Howell.**

The Toll of Justice
Fields Feature Films Company – October 1916.
Supervised by Thomas J. Peters.

Cast: **Walter Miller. Irva Ross** and possibly **William A. Howell.**

No reviews or plot are known to exist for this film

Gathem Films, Inc. - 1917 & 1918

Gathem Films, Inc. was incorporated in the State of Delaware on the 31st day of August, 1917 with William A. Howell president, W. C. Pritchard secretary, and Benjamin D. Emanuel treasurer. The total authorized capital stock of the corporation was $400,000, divided into 40,000 shares of the par value of Ten ($10.00) dollars each. The original stockholders were M. L. Rodgers, E. E. Bishop and S. F. Coursen of Wilmington, Delaware who invested $1,000 with which the corporation commenced business. The 1918 R. L. Polk's City Directory for New York City listed the Gathem Film, Inc. address as 1482 Broadway, Room 809. The following circular's listed the address as 110 West 42nd Street, New York City. William A. and Myra Howell lived at 260 Valentine Lane, Yonkers, N.Y. in 1918.

George K. Hollister, a cameraman with William A. Howell at the Thanhouser Film Corporation in 1915 and 1916, was the cameraman for Gathem Films. He was living at 325 West 51st Street, New York City during the existence of Gathem Films, Inc.

A photo of an unknown parade possibly representing the following films. (Photo from the collection of Myra Van Haden).

Gathem Films, Inc.

Our Flag, Columbia - 1918
Directed and Produced by William A. Howard,
Cinematography by George K. Hollister.

Cast: **William "Billy" Augustus Howell.**

Credits: Scenario, William A. Howell. Copyright Gathem Film Inc. (William A. Howell, author); title and description, and 21 prints, 13 June 1918; LU12561 (Unpublished Motion-Picture Photoplay).

Motion Pictures, 1912-1939.

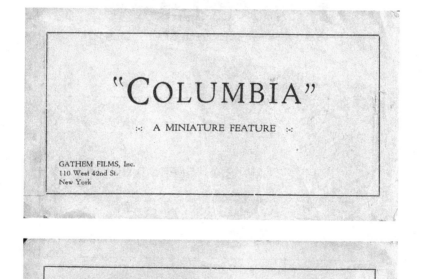

"COLUMBIA"

:·: A MINIATURE FEATURE :·:

GATHEM FILMS, Inc.
110 West 42nd St.
New York

"A visualization of our Navy Anthem of about seven minutes duration."

Produced under the direction of Wm. A. Howell

Copyright 1918

(**Circular from the collection of William D. Howard & Myra Van Haden**).

Gathem Films, Inc.

Our Flag, Columbia - 1918

(Circular from the collection of William D. Howard and Myra Van Haden).

Gathem Films, Inc.

Our Flag, Columbia - 1918

William "Billy" A. Howell filmed at Narragansett, Rhode Island.
(Photo from collection of Kathleen Howell Shallcross).

Gathem Films, Inc.

The Star Spangled Banner - 1918
Directed and Produced by William A. Howard.
Cinematography by George K. Hollister.

Cast: **Paul 'Chick' Kelly**.

Credits: Scenario, William A. Howell. Copyright Gathem Film Inc. (William A. Howell, author); title and description, 25 February 1918; 20 prints, 25 April 1918; LU12386 (Unpublished Motion-Picture Photoplay).

Motion Pictures, 1912-1939

"THE STAR SPANGLED BANNER"

:·: A MINIATURE FEATURE :·:

Produced by
GATHEM FILMS, Inc.
110 West 42nd St.
New York

"A visualization of our National Anthem of about eight minutes duration intended for the opening of all public meetings where motion pictures are exhibited."

Produced under the direction of Wm. A. Howell
and Photographed by Geo. K. Hollister

(Circular from the collection of Myra Van Haden).

118

Gathem Films, Inc.

The Star Spangled Banner - 1918

(Circular from the collection of Myra Van Haden).

Battle Cry of Freedom - 1918
Directed and Produced by William A. Howard

Credits: Scenario, W. A. Howell. Copyright Gathem Film Inc. (William A. Howell, author); title and description, 23 August 1918; 32 prints, 31 August 1918; LU12810 (Unpublished Motion-Picture Photoplay).

Motion Pictures, 1912-1939.

Home Sweet Home
August 1920.
Directed by William A. Howell.

Cast: **Daly Hunt, Milton Martinell, Doris Baker, William "Billy" Howell.**

Previewed: At the Millers and Iris Theatres.

Daly Hunt and Martin Martinell in the back row and Doris Baker and Billy Howell in front row filmed in front of Cecil B. DeMille's home. (Photo from collection of Kathy Howell Shallcross).

Trouble Brewing

Paul Gerson Pictures Corporation, San Francisco, California – 1921.
Directed by Jenny Wright.
Cinematography by George K. Hollister.

Cast: **William A. Howell** and several of his nieces.

Note: This 35mm film is in the UCLA MP Motion Picture Collection #M2505.

Short Comedy. Prohibition comedy with a dramatic actor placed in a comedian's role.

William A. Howell, with his cat, in the basement brewing.
(Photo from collection of Myra Van Haden).

Balto's Race to Nome

An Educational Special – 1 June 1925.
Produced by Sol Lesser.

If you like dogs and admire quiet heroism in humans go to see this reproduction of the race to Nome last winter. With many lives depending on dog teams to bring in diphtheria antitoxin, Gunnar Kasson and his lead dog, Balto, fight their way through sixty miles of blizzard, across ice-buried trails, to carry the serum on the last lap of its journey. A fine record of human heroism and of dog loyalty. - M.S.

Photoplay, July 1925.

Famous Alaskan Dog "Balto" and William A. Howell in studio at Hollywood. (Photo from collection Myra Van Haden).

Jesus of Nazareth

Ideal Pictures – 15 Mar 1928.
Directed by William A. Howell.
Cinematography by George K. Hollister.

Cast: **Philip Van Loan** as the Christ, **Anna Lehr** as Mary, **Charles McCaffrey** as Pontius Pilate.

Credits: Title Editor, Jean Conover; Copyrighted 15 March 1928; LP25067 (Published Motion-Picture Photoplay).

Motion Pictures, 1912-1939.

The life of the Christ from his birth, the flight into Egypt, the return to Nazareth, instructing the elders at the Temple, praying in the Garden of Gethsemane, the betrayal by Judas, the Crucifixion and his Ascension. The video gives no indication of the director, film company nor the cast.

William A. Howell in front of the camera. Filmed in New Orleans. (Photo from collection Myra Van Haden).

The Law of the Plains

Syndicate Pictures – 19 August 1929 and Produced by J. P. McGowan.

Cast: **Tom Tyler** as O'Brien, **Natalie Joyce**, **William A. Howell**, **Al Ferguson** a Naval Officer.

Western melodrama. "O'Brien (Tom Tyler), negotiating sale of his rancho, is killed by Seagrue, who takes possession under the name of Serrano. Year later, O'Brien's son, Dan, avenges his dad's death."
"Motion Picture News Booking Guide," in Motion Picture News, 15 Mar 1930, p89.

Unidentified little girl, William A. Howell and Natalie Joyce.
(Photo from collection Myra Van Haden).

Unidentified Silent Era Stills

This scene appears to have been shot at the Huddlestone Cascade in Central Park, New York City. William A. Howell and an unidentified lady. (Photo from the collection of Myra Van Haden).

The following unidentified silent movie stills seem to be related because of the markings on the stills.

William A. Howell and unidentified. Still "Dog 1."
(Photo from the collection of Myra Van Haden).

Unidentified Silent Era Stills

The following unidentified silent movie stills seem to be related because of the markings on the stills.

William A. Howell standing in front of dancers. Still "Dog 2."
(Photo from the collection of Myra Van Haden).

William A. Howell and a dog. Still "Dog 6."
(Photo from the collection of Myra Van Haden).

Unidentified Silent Era Stills

Note: The dog in the below photograph is the same dog shown in the preceding photographs.

William A. Howell and unidentified. Still "Dog 11."
(Photo from the collection of Myra Van Haden).

William A. Howell with dog at his side.
(Photo from the collection of Myra Van Haden).

Unidentified Silent Era Stills

**William A. Howell and unidentified woman standing.
(Photo from the collection of Myra Van Haden).**

William A. Howell reading. (Photo from the collection of Myra Van Haden).

Unidentified Silent Era Stills

William A. Howell, unidentified and unidentified man with cane.
(Photo from the collection of Myra Van Haden).

Leonard, unidentified, and William A. Howell.
(Photo from the collection of Myra Van Haden).

THE EMOTIONAL APPEAL

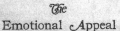

The
Emotional Appeal

An address given at the Annual
Banquet of Screen Advertisers
Association.
at The Roosevelt Hotel
By W. A. Howell
Hollywood California

THE EMOTIONAL APPEAL.

IN SPEAKING of emotion, it is necessary to keep the meaning of that word clearly fixed, otherwise one is liable to confuse it with anger, passion, excitement or any of the other mental weaknesses. Emotion, strictly speaking, is of the mind alone.

Unless we make this fine distinction, we are apt to feel a bit suspicious of the phrase "Emotional Appeal." To clarify myself and to be certain that I would apply the word correctly in my address to you, I looked up our old reliable authority, Webster. Webster defines emotion as: "to move out of, to stir up, to shake; the moving of the mind or soul." And this is the meaning I want you to keep in mind.

Benjamin Kidd, in his latest work, "The Science of Power," also applies this phrase helpful to my argument. Kidd sets out to prove that "the secret of the coming age of the world is that civilization rests not on Reason, but on Emotion."

He says, "It is through the emotional ideal, and through this cause alone, that the collec-

[Five]

(From the collection of Myra Van Haden).

THE EMOTIONAL APPEAL

tive will can be concentrated and directed to particular ends. It is through the emotion of the ideal that any collective aim whatever that the organized imagination of a people may set before itself, becomes possible of achievement, and this in an incredibly brief interval of time."

If every statesman would read that book, it might hasten the science which in the future will be a powerful force to create public opinion through the influence of the emotional ideal. This science appreciated and properly understood, would revolutionize society in a generation. There is no habit or lofty ideal that could not be inculcated in a people in a few short years if the right methods were used. One of these methods, and one in which I am chiefly interested, is that form of appeal, that sort of publicity which can be brought about by visual education.

Now, the emotional appeal pre-supposes a certain mental lethargy, faculties that need rousing before they will respond to new or neglected ideas. Sometimes a dramatic situa-

[Six]

THE EMOTIONAL APPEAL

tion is sufficient to do it, such as war, or some other, lesser national disaster. The appeal lies in the event itself, which is sufficiently dynamic to stir men's minds. But sometimes, and generally, the appeal must be organized, set before the people in such a way that their sympathies are roused and their minds react to the stimulation of that deep-seated part of their nature touching the ideal.

You know what I mean.

When a country is in danger, the people will give unstinted service to the State. The emotional appeal is so instantaneous, so overwhelming that undreamed-of heroism becomes almost commonplace. The people's minds and souls have been so touched, shaken up, stirred, moved out of their customary grooves, that nobility of purpose governs their action and no demand for self-sacrifice seems too great.

Such appeal will turn men and women from cold reason, which governs SELF-regarding actions, to emotion, which generates OTHER-regarding ideas.

[Seven]

THE EMOTIONAL APPEAL

You clearly see the application.

But human nature is very fallible. Unless it is fed, recreated and continually galvanized, the most idealistic emotion peters out; nor can it ever become a permanent idea with the great majority unless by actual visual contact the lesson or appeal is brought into their inner consciousness. This visual appeal lies in the organized scientific publicity with which you are all familiar and in sympathy, the Motion Picture.

Despite the fact that the making of motion pictures is a great industry, in fact, the third largest in the United States, it is nevertheless to-day, at its best, experimental,—a crude, faint hint of what it easily might become to morrow when used in the supremely important business of education.

The invention of printing and the subsequent advent of the newspaper in 1632 was of secondary significance in comparison with the introduction of the first flickering, buzzing, jerky "movie" in 1896. The newspaper has stirred

[Eight]

THE EMOTIONAL APPEAL

men's minds, but the motion picture can stir their minds and touch their hearts;—and there is nothing more powerful than the emotional appeal.

What one sees is remembered, what one hears or reads is often forgotten.

Moving pictures already play an important part in the lives of all people, although at present it is chiefly for entertainment; but once education becomes tied-up with entertainment, it will become a mighty educative force.

Scholars and philosophers may sit in their studies and get all the inspiration they need from their books; but others, less well-educated, those with hard lives, little imagination, and no historical sense, must be led by new and easy paths to the knowledge they ought to possess. When education, historic or other scientific facts, shapes itself into a series of dramatic scenes that hold the onlookers spellbound, and leave their minds deeply impressed with certain facts, then we may hope to be able to allay much of the suffering of hu-

[Nine]

(From the collection of Myra Van Haden).

131

THE EMOTIONAL APPEAL

manity primarily due to misunderstanding of facts and ignorance. Thousands of babies die every year because of the ignorance of those who give them birth and bring them up. And think of the host of our younger generation who rush into marriage relations without even the slightest knowledge of sex hygiene.

Surely much of this blindness and its attendant misery is preventable. We have in the motion picture the means by which knowledge can be given to the millions in a cheap, easily understood, lively and dramatic form — — and it is time we turned it to account! The motion picture can be made entertaining where the teacher, lecturer or reformer is almost always dull. It can make a silent appeal to one's emotions far more touching than the most eloquent speech.

Very soon every State and County will use motion picture propaganda, and the Board of Education and the Board of Health will be the first to lead the way. Their work is so closely tied up with the well-being of the community that there are hardly any arguments necessary.

[Ten]

THE EMOTIONAL APPEAL

Imagine the germ theory dramatically treated, with just the right tinge of repulsion and humor to drive home the lesson on hygiene or sanitation such as the onlookers couldn't forget; what a compelling film that would be! And another on physical culture, leaving the audience craving to possess such beauty, symmetry, health and grace as the picture suggested were possible.

The Farm Bureau and its affiliation, as well as the various large and legitimate land agencies, will distribute motion pictures telling an interesting and appealing story of other farming communities, the opportunities they offer to immigrants and those seeking different environments in other States, the sort of homes, climate, scenery, wages and so on, they may expect.

I see the motion picture replace the blackboard in the schools. Knowledge without boredom is what the motion pictures could offer under the right auspices, the sort of knowledge that would help to make a nation of healthy, contented, right-thinking people,

[Eleven]

THE EMOTIONAL APPEAL

INFORMED as no other whole nation has ever been yet.

Suppose all history was taught through the motion picture, so that the people learned to love and understand their heritage. Suppose the great historical figures that are so tedious and incomprehensible to children were made, seemingly, to live and move before their eyes, costumes, eccentricities, pageantry, plots and counterplots complete. Suppose we could watch the lives and struggles of the world's big men and women, and mark their patience and nobility?

A great deal has already been done with films along those lines, but there remains much more to do. Especially do we want more of the customs, manners, dress, homes and ideals of our own peoples filmed and produced. Our country's history with its pageantry, legends, the story of its great men and women,—what an impression that would leave on our minds!

We want to see the progress of our industries linked up with the progress of our coun-

[Twelve]

THE EMOTIONAL APPEAL

try. Short entertaining moving pictures, depicting the romance of science and industries— that is what is wanted by the public and the big film distributing corporations of our country. We are a very inquisitive people, we want to see behind the scenes, watch the struggles and achievements of our country's industries. We don't want to know their trade secrets, but we do want to see "the works," the mechanical or scientific methods which they use to create or manufacture their particular merchandise. Industrial pictures should be governed by the idea of service, the influence of which would reach to the very hearth-stone of the community—the family.

What greater medium is there to-day to accomplish this than the motion picture with its EMOTIONAL APPEAL?

[Thirteen]

(From the collection of Myra Van Haden).

132

HOLLYWOOD

After the introduction of sound motion pictures William A. Howell was known and credited as Anders Van Haden. I have attempted to list all of his known movies, their descriptions and have included movie stills where existing.

The identification of most of these movie stills was made from the studio identification on the photographs. The studio marking on the stills normally referred to the director of that film and the descriptions given in The Motion Picture Guide helped in the identification of the still from that motion picture. For example, "McFad-8-7" was found to be a still from "Cheaters at Play" directed by Hamilton McFadden.

Many of the films listed were also identified from the various citations listed on the following pages along with a list that Myra Van Haden had enclosed with a scrapbook of movie stills that she left with her grandchildren. Some of the citations indicate variations of the spelling of Anders Van Haden and one citation noting W. A. Howell.

Studio stills from the German language versions of "The Big Trail" (Die Grosse Fahrt), "The Big House" (Menschen Hinter Gittern), "Laurel-Hardy Murder Case" (Der Spuk um Mitternacht), and "Hollywood Revue of 1929" (Wir Schalten um auf Hollywood), are probably shown here for the first time.

Anders Van Haden Standard Casting Directory Listing,
(From collection of Myra Van Haden).

Hollywood

The International Film Reporter

ANDERS VAN HADEN'S 7 GERMAN TALKIES

Anders van Haden is holding the distinction of having played featured parts in 7 German talkies made in Hollywood: his "Flack" in Fox's "Grosse Fahrt," (Big Trail) is according to Director Lew Seiler an incomparably outstanding characterization. Van Haden, an American, speaks German like a native; no wonder he was cast in "Mordprozess Mary Dugan", "Maske Faellt", Daemon des Meeres", "Wir schalten um auf Hollywood", and lately in "Menschen hinter Gittern". An actor of van Haden's fine diction and acting ability is always in demand.

Date unknown.

Performing Arts Biography Master Index

VanHaden, Anders 1876-1936 WhScrn, WhoHol

WhScrn   Who Was Who on Screen
WhoHol   Who's Who in Hollywood, 1900-1976

The Motion Picture Guide

W. A. Howell
FIGHTING MARSHALL, THE (1932)

Anders Van Haden
CHEATERS AT PLAY (1932); BEST OF ENEMIES (1933); SECRET OF THE BLUE ROOM (1933); MADAME SPY (1934); WE LIVE AGAIN (1934); BARBARY COAST (1935); FOLIES BERGERE (1935)

Anders Van Hayden
    PASSPORT TO HELL (1932)

Anders Von Haden
    STAMBOUL QUEST (1934)

The New York Times Directory of the Film

Van Haden, Anders
    Cheaters at Play 1932, F 27,22:1
    Passport to Hell, A 1932, Ag 27,13:4
    Best of Enemies 1933, Jl 17,19:5
    Secret of the Blue Room, The 1933, S 13,22:1
    Barbary Coast 1935, O 14,21:1

Hollywood

Who's Who in Hollywood, 1900 - 1976

VAN HADEN, ANDERS (1936) 60 - Support in several of the 30's: Edward G. Robinson's Barbary Coast (as Second Mate), Lionel Atwill's Secret of the Blue Room, Paul Lukas' Passport to Hell, etc.

Who Was Who on Screen

VAN HADEN, ANDERS

Born 1876. Died: June 19, 1936, Hollywood, Calif (heart attack). Screen actor, film producer, and film director.

Appeared in: 1932 Cheaters at Play; A Passport to Hell. 1933 Best of Enemies; The Secret of the Blue Room; Snug in the Jug (short). 1935 Barbary Coast.

International Film Necrology

Van Haden, Anders, actor; d. June 19, 1936 (60).

The 1933 Film Daily Year Book of Motion Pictures

PLAYERS' WORK

HOWELL, W. A.
(1932) Fighting Marshall

VAN HADEN, ANDERS
(1932) Cheaters at Play, Passport to Hell.

The 1934 Film Daily Year Book of Motion Pictures

PLAYERS' WORK

HOWELL, W. A.
(1932) Fighting Marshall

VAN HADEN, ANDERS
(1932) Cheaters at Play, Passport to Hell.
(1933) Best of Enemies, Secret of the Blue Room.

Hollywood

American Film Institute Catalog, 1931–1940

Howell, W. A.
1931   The Fighting Marshall

Van Haden, Anders aka Haden,
Anders van; Von Haden, Anders
1931   Die Maske Fällt
          The Spider
1932   Cheaters at Play
          A Passport to Hell
1933   Best of Enemies
          Secret of the Blue Room
1934   Little Man, What Now?
          Love Time
          Madame Spy
          Riptide
          Stamboul Quest
          We Live Again
          The World Moves On
1935   The Affair of Susan
          Barbary Coast
          Bride of Frankenstein
          The County Chairman
          The Daring Young Man
          Diamond Jim
          The Florentine Dagger
          Folies Bergére de Paris
          Les Misérables
          Mystery Woman
          Thunder in the Night
1936   Desert Gold
          The Story of Louis Pasteur

Motion Picture Production Guide - 1936

PLAYERS AND THEIR AGENTS' TELEPHONES

Van Haden, Anders .... **Hollywood 1045**
I. M. Sackin, 6605 Hollywood Blvd, Hollywood, California

Sound Films, 1927 - 1939, A United States Filmography

Van Haden, Anders

225.	Barbary Coast (1935)
286.	The Best of Enemies (1933)
473.	The Bride of Frankenstein (1935)
692.	Cheaters at Play (1932)
3500.	A Passport to Hell (1932)
4049.	Secret of the Blue Room (1933)

Hollywood

Foreign Language Film Production in Hollywood

La Voz Ibero-Americana, Por Minerva Del Castillo

Production of foreign language pictures, on the basis of picture for picture with English speaking talkies, will be underway within a month at the Metro-Goldwyn-Mayer studios, it was announced recently by Arthur Loew, in charge of the company's affairs outside of the United States, and now in California to confer with Louis B. Mayer, Irving G. Thalber and other production heads.

The announcement means fifty foreign language pictures to be made during the coming year, in addition to the regular American productions. The majority of these will be in French, German and Spanish. The schedule will more than double the total output of the studio. It means the importation of many new construction and other development.

Loew, vice-president in charge of the Metro-Goldwyn-Mayer European interests, states that reception of American made foreign language pictures in other lands in the past year made the new production program imperative.

"With the strong nucleus of non-English stars, directors and writers now at the studios," he stated, "and the addition of a very considerable number recently signed abroad and about to leave for Hollywood, we will be ready in one month to embark on the plan of foreign picture production paralleling our domestic schedule. It means also production of short subjects on a similar scale."

Permanent stock companies in foreign languages will be organized for the plan, according to Loew. "These, he states, "will be well-rounded units, complete in themselves in acting, writing and directing personnel, and will, moreover, have the benefit of the advice and assistance of our American directors and technicians. Of course, the entire mechanical equipment of the studio will be at the service of the foreign units."

There are forty-four French, German and Italian players and writers now under contract to the studio. Through arrangements made by Ludwig Lawrence, M-G-M's special representative, to this contract list will be added during the coming month Lya Lys, French actress; Roger Ferdinand, French playwright; Louis Branel and Leon Burgiers, French directors; Maria Ladron de Guevara and Maria Tubau, Spanish actresses, and some six other celebrities; Mona Goya, French actress, and Julia Peña Spanish stage star recently arrived.

Foreign production activity at present at the studio includes "Toto" with Ernesto Vilches in Spanish and a German picture with Nora Gregor, Egon von Jordan, Paul Morgan and Adolphe Menjou, and in which a number of American stars will appear. Buster Keaton is filming "Free and Easy" in German, Ramon Navarro is directing and starring in "Call of the Flesh" in French, and Grace Moore is doing a French version of "A Lady's

Morals," based on the life of Jenny Lind. Miss Moore is to do another foreign language film on completion of this.

Among the short subjects, the "All Barkie" two reelers, the Hal Roach comedies, including Charley Chase, Laurel and Hardy, and other features, are being released in several languages, and to meet a new demand, feature length comedies with the Roach stars are planned.

"Until six months ago the percentage of houses wired for sound was small in foreign countries" states Loew, "but now, and in South America particularly, there has been a tremendous jump in sound installations."

"Audiences, at first satisfied to hear favorite American stars speak in English, now demand a product they can understand and of a quality with the American. It is to meet this our demand that we are working out the new schedule. Already some of our foreign pictures have proven outstanding hits, and their reception has shown us that the new production plan is not only justified but is a necessity."

Loew's conference with the Culver City studio heads worked out full details of the new foreign production schedule. He will remain at the studio some days to see the working out of the new plan, before returning to Europe to prepare for the new season there.

November 8, 1930, Hollywood Filmograph.

Mamba
Tiffany Productions – 10 March 1930.
Directed by Albert S. Rogell.

Cast: **Jean Hersholt** as August Bolte/Mamba, **Eleanor Boardman** as **Helen von Linden**, **Ralph Forbes** as Karl von Reiden, **Anders Van Haden** as General Liebreich, **Josef Swickhard** as Count von Linden.

This film concerns Zulus in Africa, the end of World War I, and the tale of Hersholt. Hersholt takes his bride that he brought to Africa and gets entangled with the warring tribes. Shooting in the color process throughout the film was a formidable job at the same time when even sound was a big deal.

The Motion Picture Guide.

Anders Van Haden on the left. (Photo from collection of Myra Van Haden).

Die Maske Fällt
Warner's First National - 5 February 1931.
(German language version of *The Way of All Men*).
Directed by William Dieterle.

Cast: **Lissi Arna, Anton Pointer, Karl Etlinger, Carla Bartheel, Ulrich Steindorff, Arno Frey, Leon Janney, Charlotte Hagenbruch, Anders Van Haden** as Dick Stratton, **Salka Steuremann**.

Billy Bear allies himself with the wealthy Swift and make millions in the market, then goes to a basement speakeasy in New Orleans to arrange a victory party. Present at the illegal watering-hole are a variety of wealthy people, bums, and shady ladies such as Bear's one-time love interest Poppy, a former actress and now a woman of the streets. The flood waters of the Mississippi River threaten to burst a levee an inundate the establishment, so quick-thinking proprietor Stratton closes the airtight doors of the gin mill (doors installed for just an eventuality). Billy Baer recants his rejection of Poppy and prepares to die with her, finally demanding that the doors be opened to let the floodwaters take them. The doors are indeed opened, and lo, the sun is shining: the levee didn't give way after all!

The Motion Picture Guide (American Version).

Der Dämon Meeres

Warner Bros. - 12 March 1931.
(German language version of *Moby Dick*).
Directed by Michael Curtiz [Kertesz].

Cast: **William Dieterle** as Captain Ahab, **Lissi Arna** as Faith, **Anton Pointer, Karl Etlinger, Carla Bartheel, Lothar Mayring, Bert Sprotte, Otto Kottke, Reginald Pasch, Anders Van Haden** as Stubbs, The Mate; **John Eskridge, Adolph Milar.**

The story has Dieterle and the evil stepbrother battling over the affections of the preacher's daughter. On a whaling voyage the stepbrother shoves Ahab overboard into the maw of the great white title whale, which bites his leg off. The stump is cauterized on the deck as Ahab screams and several men sit on him to hold him down. Twisted by pain and the loss of his leg, Ahab returns home. When Arna sees the frightening figure, she naturally recoils in shock and runs away. Ahab takes this as proof of what his brother has been hinting, that Faith doesn't love him anymore. The peg-legged sea captain leaves home again, obsessed with killing Moby Dick. After seven years of searching the whale is located and killed, Ahab driving home the harpoon. The brother gets his comeuppance, leaving Ahab free to return to New Bedford and Faith. In many ways the film does not hold up today, owing to its ludicrous plot complete with evil stepbrother right out of 19th-Century melodrama and a fake whale that won't fool anyone (although the life-sized rubber model is more convincing than that used in the 1926 version).

The Motion Picture Guide (American Version).

John Barrymore was Captain Ahab, Joan Bennett was *Faith* and *Stubbs*, the mate, was played by Walter Long in the American release of Moby Dick.

Mordprozess Mary Dugan
MGM - 1931.
(German language version of *Trial of Mary Dugan*).
Directed by Arthur Robison.

Cast: **Nora Gregor** as Mary Dugan, **Arnold Korff, Julia Serda, Egon von Jordan, Peter Erkelenz, Anders Van Haden** as Inspector Hunt.

Metro-Goldwyn-Mayer production and Parufamet release. Berlin, Feb. 20, 1931.

In Germany the all dialog film has again dropped before it really reached the stage of perfection. This splendid and thrilling American stage hit proved at the Berlin premiere that it in no way lost anything on the screen in this foreign version. In spite of its length the audience remained at attention.

Bad casting and ignorance of the German taste have been avoided. Nora Gregor, as Mary Dugan, is gripping in certain scenes, while Arnold Korff was liked. Julia Serda, in a smaller role this time, shows her splendid qualities, but Egon von Jordan, as the brother, at times still overplays.

Sound reproduction is distinct, and the German dialog to the point and tense. Film promises good box office returns over here.

Variety, March 4, 1931.

Anders signed a standard artists contract with MGM Studios on July 28, 1930 for $250.00 per week for the role of *Inspector Hunt* in the photoplay of the German Language Version of Trial of Mary Dugan.

Mordprozess Mary Dugan

𝕸𝖎𝖓𝖎𝖒𝖚𝖒 𝕮𝖔𝖓𝖙𝖗𝖆𝖈𝖙 𝖋𝖔𝖗 𝕬𝖗𝖙𝖎𝖘𝖙𝖘

CONTINUOUS EMPLOYMENT—WEEKLY BASIS—WEEKLY SALARY
ONE WEEK MINIMUM EMPLOYMENT
Effective March 1, 1930

METRO-GOLDWYN-MAYER STUDIOS

CALL BUREAU

THIS AGREEMENT made this ......28th...... day of ......July...... , 193.0., between

..................METRO-GOLDWYN-MAYER CORPORATION...................; (hereinafter called "producer") and

...................Anders van Haden..................., (hereinafter called "artist").

WITNESSETH:

1. The producer hereby engages the artist to render services as such in the role of ......Inspector Hunt......
in a photoplay the working title of which is now "......German Version-Trial of Mary Dugan......"
at a salary of ......Two Hundred and fifty......Dollars ($ ......250.00......) per week. The artist
accepts said engagement upon the terms herein specified.

2. The term of employment hereunder shall begin on or about the ......28th...... day of ......July...... , 193.0.
and shall continue thereafter until the completion of the photographing and/or recordation of said role. If after the expiration of the
term hereof the producer should desire the services of the artist in making retakes, or in making added scenes, or in making any
"transparencies" or trick shots, or in making "trailers," or in making any change or changes in said photoplay, or in making any
foreign version or versions of said photoplay, then and in either of said events, the artist agrees to render such services in connection
therewith as and when the producer may request, unless the artist is otherwise employed, but if otherwise employed the artist will
cooperate to the fullest extent in the making of such retakes, added scenes, "transparencies," trick shots, "trailers," changes, and/or
foreign versions. Services in connection with retakes, added scenes, "transparencies," trick shots, "trailers," changes, and/or foreign
versions, if such services are commenced within six (6) months after the expiration of the term hereof, shall be upon the same terms
and at the same rate of compensation as herein set forth, such compensation to be paid from the time when the artist's services are
first rendered in connection with such retakes, added scenes, "transparencies," trick shots, "trailers," changes, and/or foreign versions,
until the completion of the artist's services in connection therewith. The phrase "on or about" as hereinabove used shall allow a
latitude of forty-eight (48) hours (exclusive of Sundays and holidays) either prior to or after the date hereinabove specified as the
commencement of the term hereof; it being agreed that the exact date for the commencement of the term hereof is to be specified by
the producer and is to be not earlier than forty-eight (48) hours before the date hereinabove specified, nor later than forty-eight (48)
hours after the date hereinabove specified (exclusive of Sundays and holidays). The term "role" as used in this agreement shall be
deemed to refer to said role as now written and/or as it may from time to time hereafter be rewritten and/or lengthened and/or
shortened by the producer in the exercise of its sole discretion and judgment.

3. The artist agrees to be prompt in appearing for work as required by the producer, to perform services hereunder in a
conscientious and painstaking manner and in accordance with the reasonable instructions of the producer, and to abide by the reasonable
studio rules and regulations of the producer. The producer shall have the exclusive right to the services of the artist during the term
hereof, and the artist agrees that during the term hereof the artist will not render any services of any kind to or for any person, firm,
or corporation other than the producer without first obtaining the express written consent of the producer.

4. The term "photoplay" as used in this agreement shall be deemed to include motion pictures produced and/or exhibited with
sound and voice recording, reproducing and/or transmitting devices, radio devices, and all other improvements and devices which are
now or may hereafter be used in connection with the production and/or exhibition and/or transmission of any present or future kind of
motion picture production. The producer shall have the right to photograph and/or otherwise produce, reproduce, transmit, exhibit,
distribute, and exploit in connection with said photoplay any and all of the artist's acts, poses, plays and appearances of any and
all kinds hereunder, and shall further have the right to record, reproduce, transmit, exhibit, distribute, and exploit in connection with
said photoplay the artist's voice, and all instrumental, musical, and other sound effects produced by the artist in connection with
such acts, poses, plays and appearances. The producer shall likewise have the right to use and give publicity to the artist's name
and likeness, photographic or otherwise, and to recordations and reproductions of the artist's voice and all instrumental, musical, and
other sound effects produced by the artist hereunder, in connection with the advertising and exploitation of said photoplay. The rights
in this paragraph granted to the producer shall inure to the benefit not only of the producer, but also to the benefit of all persons who
may hereafter acquire from the producer any right to distribute, transmit, exhibit, advertise, or exploit said photoplay.

5. The producer agrees that it will not "dub" or use a "double" in lieu of the artist, except under the following circumstances:
(a) when necessary to expeditiously meet the requirements of foreign exhibition; (b) when necessary to expeditiously meet censorship
requirements, both foreign and domestic; (c) when, in the opinion of the producer, the failure to use a "double" for the performance
of hazardous acts might result in physical injury to the artist; (d) when the artist is not available; and (e) when the artist fails or is
unable to meet certain requirements of the role, such as singing or the rendition of instrumental music or other similar services
requiring special talent or ability other than that possessed by the artist. The artist does hereby agree that under either or any of
the conditions hereinabove in subdivisions (a) to (e), both inclusive, of this paragraph 5 set forth, the producer shall have the right to
"double" and/or "dub" not only the acts, poses, plays and appearances of the artist, but also the voice of the artist, and all instrumental,
musical, and other sound effects to be produced by the artist, to such extent as may be required by the producer.

6. Where the services of the artist are required to be performed outside of the City of Los Angeles or its environs, the producer
shall transport the artist and the reasonable personal baggage of the artist, and pay all necessary traveling expenses of the artist,
including reasonable charges for board and lodging.

7. If the production of said photoplay be necessarily prevented, suspended, or postponed during the course of production, by
reason of fire, accident, strike, riot, act of God, or of the public enemy, or by any executive or judicial order, no salary need be paid the
artist for the first week's prevention, suspension, or postponement. If the production of said photoplay be prevented, suspended, or
postponed by reason of the illness of any other member of the cast or of the director, full salary shall be paid the artist for the first
week's prevention, suspension, or postponement. It shall be the duty of the producer during the first week of any prevention,
suspension, or postponement to notify the artist in writing whether the producer will entirely discontinue the production or further
suspend or postpone it, and in the latter event the producer shall pay the artist half salary during such further suspended or postponed
period. At the end of five (5) weeks from the date on which the producer has stopped production the artist may terminate this
employment if the artist so elects, unless the producer continues thereafter to pay the artist full weekly compensation. If the
production of said photoplay is prevented, suspended, or postponed for any reason hereinabove in this paragraph provided, then and
in that event the producer may terminate this employment at any time after the commencement of such prevention, suspension, or
postponement. If the producer elect to terminate this employment by reason of the illness of any other member of the cast or of the
director, then the producer shall be obligated to pay the artist such balance, if any, as is then unpaid for services theretofore rendered
by the artist, and also one week's compensation, upon the payment of which the producer shall be discharged of and from all liability
whatsoever hereunder. If such termination be based on the happening of any other cause hereinabove in this paragraph set forth,
then the producer shall be obligated to pay the artist only such balance, if any, as is then unpaid for services theretofore rendered by
the artist, and upon the payment of such unpaid balance, if any, the producer shall be discharged of and from all liability whatsoever
hereunder. The producer need pay no salary during any period that the artist is incapacitated, by illness or otherwise, from performing
the required services hereunder, and in the event of such illness or incapacity the producer, at its option, may terminate this
employment without further liability.

8. The artist agrees to furnish all modern wardrobe and wearing apparel reasonably necessary for the portrayal of said
role; it being agreed, however, that should so-called "character" or "period" costumes be required the producer shall supply the same.
Any loss of or damage to costumes, wardrobe, and other property furnished by the artist necessarily arising through the performance
of the artist's services, or through lack of due care on the part of the producer, shall be paid for by the producer to the artist. All
costumes, wardrobe, and other property furnished by the producer shall belong to the producer and be returned promptly to it, and any
loss of or damage thereto arising through lack of due care on the part of the artist, or not necessarily arising through the performance
of the artist's services, shall be paid for by the artist to the producer. Any loss of or damage to wardrobe, for which either party hereto
may be liable, shall be computed on the basis of depreciation schedules to be furnished from time to time by the American Appraisal
Company.

**MGM Minimum Contract for Artists. (From
the collection of Myra Van Haden).**

Mordprozess Mary Dugan

9. The producer may terminate the artist's employment at any time, either prior to the commencement of production of said photoplay or during the course of production; provided, however, that if the producer elect to terminate the artist's employment hereunder more than thirty (30) days prior to the starting date hereinabove in paragraph 2 specified, then and in that event the producer shall be free from all liability of every kind whatsoever; but provided further that if the producer elect to terminate the artist's employment hereunder at any time within thirty (30) days prior to said starting date, or at any time thereafter, or during the course of production of said photoplay, the producer shall be obligated to pay the artist such balance, if any, as is then unpaid for services theretofore rendered by the artist, and also one week's compensation, upon the payment of which the producer shall be discharged of and from all liability whatsoever hereunder, subject, however, to the provisions of paragraphs 7 and 11 hereof.

10. If during the first or last week of the artist's employment hereunder the artist shall have actually appeared before the camera or been on call less than six (6) full days, then the artist's salary for such week shall be prorated, and for this purpose one day's salary shall be one-sixth (1/6) of the weekly rate. If the services of the artist at the commencement of the term hereof are to be rendered at a place which can be reached from the producer's studio within twenty-four (24) hours of travel by ordinary means of transportation, then and in that event compensation shall not begin to accrue to the artist until the artist's first appearance before the camera at such place or until the artist is first put on call at such place; provided, however, that in any event compensation must commence to accrue to the artist not later than forty-eight (48) hours after such place; provided, however, that in any event compensation shall accrue to the artist during the time reasonably required to return the artist to Los Angeles. If the services of the artist at the commencement of the term hereof are to be rendered at a place which cannot be reached from the producer's studio within twenty-four (24) hours of travel by ordinary means of transportation, then and in that event compensation shall not commence to accrue to the artist during such travel period and prior to the artist's first appearance before the camera at such place, or prior to the time when the artist is first put on call at such place; provided, however, that in any event compensation must commence to accrue to the artist not later than forty-eight (48) hours after such place has been reached; and compensation shall accrue to the artist during the time reasonably required to return the artist to Los Angeles. A week shall be deemed to start at 12:01 a.m. on Thursday and end at 12 o'clock midnight of the succeeding Wednesday. If, during any week the artist shall have actually appeared before the camera or been on call each day, the artist shall receive one day's additional compensation for the services rendered by the artist on Sunday, and for this purpose, also, one day's salary shall be one-sixth (1/6) of the weekly rate. Compensation to the artist hereunder shall be payable on Saturday for services rendered up to and including the preceding Wednesday.

11. The producer guarantees that it will furnish the artist not less than _____ (_____) weeks' employment hereunder; and if the foregoing blank is not filled in, then the producer shall be deemed to have agreed to guarantee to the artist that it will furnish the artist not less than one (1) week's employment hereunder. The guarantee in this paragraph 11 set forth shall be subject, of course, to the rights of suspension and termination hereinabove in paragraph 7 granted to the producer. The producer agrees, that upon request of the artist, it will advise the artist, if and when able to do so, of the estimated date on which, in the opinion of the producer, the artist's employment hereunder will terminate, it being understood, of course, that such estimated date of termination shall not be binding on the producer, but that the producer in good faith and to the best of its ability will endeavor to advise the artist of such estimated date of termination as far in advance of the actual date of termination as the producer may be able to estimate the same.

12. If the artist shall be dismissed for the day, the artist shall not thereafter be recalled for work within a period of less than twelve (12) hours after the time of such dismissal for the day.

13. If this agreement is not executed by the producer and available for delivery to the artist at the producer's studio, or if the same is not executed by the producer and mailed to the artist, on or before the close of business on the next succeeding business day after this agreement has been executed by the artist, then this agreement, at the option of the artist, shall be null and void. Should the artist elect to exercise the right of termination under the provisions of this paragraph 13, the artist must do so by written notice to be served upon the producer before twelve (12) o'clock, noon, of the second business day after the execution hereof by the artist.

14. All notices which the producer is required or may desire to give to the artist may be given either by mailing the same addressed to the artist personally, either orally or in writing, _____ Los Angeles, California, or such notice may be given to the artist personally, either orally or in writing.

15. THE ARTIST MUST KEEP THE PRODUCER'S CASTING OFFICE OR THE ASSISTANT DIRECTOR OF SAID PHOTOPLAY ADVISED AS TO WHERE THE ARTIST MAY BE REACHED BY TELEPHONE WITHOUT UNREASONABLE DELAY.

16. Should any dispute or controversy arise between the parties hereto with reference to this contract or the employment herein provided for, such dispute or controversy shall be referred for a termination to a committee consisting of five foundation members of the Actors' Branch of the Academy of Motion Picture Arts and Sciences, which committee is to be selected by the Executive Committee of the Actors' Branch of said Academy of Motion Picture Arts and Sciences. Either party to such arbitration may appeal from the decision rendered by such committee, and in such event the dispute or controversy between the parties hereto shall be determined by the Conciliation Committee of said Academy of Motion Picture Arts and Sciences. Any arbitration hereunder shall be conducted in accordance with the by-laws of said Academy of Motion Picture Arts and Sciences, and in accordance with such rules as may from time to time be formulated by said Academy of Motion Picture Arts and Sciences.

IN WITNESS WHEREOF, the parties hereto have executed this agreement the day and year first above written.

Starting on Salary July 28, 1930

METRO-GOLDWYN-MAYER CORPORATION,
(Producer)

By _____
(Vice President)

_____
(Artist)

Casting Director _____

This Minimum Contract to be administered through the Academy of Motion Picture Arts and Sciences has been established by a Basic Agreement signed by a large majority of representative artists in Los Angeles and by the company members of the Association of Motion Picture Producers, Inc., to be effective for a period of five years from March 1, 1930, subject to revisions as provided in said Basic Agreement.

MGM Minimum Contract for Artists. (From the collection of Myra Van Haden).

Die Grosse Fahrt
Fox – 2 June 1931.
(German language version of *The Big Trail*).
Directed by Lewis Seiler and Produced by Raoul Walsh.

Cast: **Theo Shall** as Bill Coleman, **Marion Lessing** as Ruth Winter, **Ulrich Haupt** as Thorpe, **Arnold Korff** as Peter, and **Anders Van Haden** as Red Flack.

Anders Van Haden as Red Flack.
(Photo from collection of Myra Van Haden).

Die Grosse Fahrt

Fox production and Deutsche Fox-Film A. G. release. Berlin, April 9, 1930.

Press reports and reports of Americans gave hope for something good. As far as the German version is concerned, they are not justified.

Overwhelming and beautiful pictures of tremendous buffalo hers, vast steppes and snow clad mountains, the inhuman and terrible difficulties the pioneers had to cope with, beautifully illustrated by Raoul Walsh, all is diminished by the clumsy German dialog and haphazard scenes. Unnecessary German captions prolong the picture. And still this talker is most impressive by its vastness of scene and gigantic idea. Invariably one is reminded of the silent "Covered Wagon."

Diversity of opinions of the premiere audience was mostly due to the primitive dialog and acting. Many of the scenes are good stage acting; others, though, something far worse. It is hard to say has done much better work in other German versions, and most likely the same applies to the other actors. It is difficult to predict the box-office success of this talker. It most likely will give returns in rural Germany.

Variety, April 22, 1931.

Anders Van Haden on horseback. (Photo from collection of Myra Van Haden).

Die Grosse Fahrt

Note: **John Wayne** was Breck Coleman, **Marguerite Churchill** was Ruth Coleman and **Tyron Power, Sr.** played Red Flack in American release of The Big Trail.

Unidentified and Anders Van Haden. (Photos from collection of Myra Van Haden).

Menschen Hinter Gittern

MGM - 2 October 1931 (Netherlands).
(German language version of *The Big House*).
Directed by Paul Fejos.

Cast: **Heinrich George** as Butch, **Gustav Diessl** as Morris, **Dita Parlo** as Annie Marlow, **Hans Heinrich Von Twardowski** as Oliver, **Egon von Jordan** as Kent Marlow, **Anton Pointer** as Guard Wallace, **Anders Van Haden** as Sandy, **Karl Etlinger** as a Prison Guard, **Paul Morgan** as Putnam.

One of the most successful prison films ever produced, The Big House follows three inmates John Morgan, Butch Schmidt, and Kent Marlowe, a forger, a killer, and a rather innocuous youth convicted of manslaughter. Morgan escape, going to Marlowe's sister, Ann, for aid, falling in love with her before he is recaptured and returned to prison, vowing to go straight. Butch is the top bull con, settling fights and running the yard; he plans a big break to escape the sadistic guards and the endless stoolpigeons. But weak-willed Marlowe informs warden James Adams of the impending escape attempt and when Butch and other inmates make their play, they are met by horrific gunfire. It's a battle royal where Marlowe is killed, as is Butch, cut to pieces by machine-gun fire. Morgan finally restores order in the prison block, for which he is paroled so that he join Ann. Grimly realistic, often brutal, this was the granddaddy of all prison films, exposing the mean conditions, the paranoia, the vicious system that deepened criminal resolves among inmates. The film was inspired by a particularly bloody riot in Auburn (New York) prison a year earlier.

The Motion Picture Guide (American Version).

Heinrich George and Anders Van Haden standing at the right.
(Courtesy of MGM Collection at the Academy of
Motion Picture Arts and Sciences).

Wir Schalten um auf Hollywood
MGM - 10 June 1931 Germany).
(German language version of *Hollywood Revue of 1929*).
Directed by Frank Reicher.

Cast: **Adolphe Menjou, Heinrich George, Dita Parlo, Nora Gregor, Paul Morgan** as themselves, **Anders Van Haden** as The Heavenly Judge.

The American version was designed as The Hollywood Revue of 1929 (AKA The March of Time), and was given up as hopeless when near completion. It was finally released as Broadway to Hollywood/Ring Up the Curtain in 1933 with all but a smidgen of the revue jettisoned, but with a dramatic story developed from the original show-business-through-the-years idea.

The MGM Story.

Center Judge is Anders Van Haden with Adolphe Menjou standing and Heinrich George at the far right. (Photo from collection of Myra Van Haden).

Der Spuk um Mitternacht
MGM - 21 May 1931 Germany).
(German language version of *The Laurel and Hardy Murder Case*).
Directed by James Parrott and Produce by Hal Roach.

Cast: **Stan Laurel, Oliver Hardy** as themselves, **Dorothy Granger** as the Furious Woman, **Stanley Blystone** and **Anders Van Haden** as Detectives, **Otto Fries** as the Conductor, **Tiny Sandford** as a Policeman.

Foreign language versions in French (*Feu Mon Oncle*), in Spanish (*Noche de Duendes*), and in German (*Der Spuk um Mitternacht*) were shot at the same time as the English version. The German version was re-titled (*Nachtmerries*) for Dutch release Dorothy Granger (outraged young lady) appeared in all three foreign language versions. The foreign language versions are longer by one reel which included a train trip to the mansion. According to the studio payroll ledger, Anders Van Haden was paid $35.00 on each of the following four days - May 21, 22, 23 and 24, 1930. The preceding information and the following studio still identification is the courtesy of the Hal Roach Collection, Doheny Library, University of Southern California.

Eine Szene aus dem letzten Laurel und Hardy Lustspiel "DER SPUK UM MITTERNACHT". Eine Hal Roach Produktion in deutscher Sprache, im Verleih von Metro Goldwyn Mayer.

Oliver Hardy, Tiny Sandford, Anders Van Haden, Otto Fries, Stan Laurel, with Stanley Blystone behind Stan Laurel. (Photo from collection of Myra Van Haden).

The Spider

Fox - 27 September 1931.
Directed by William C. Menzies and Kenneth MacKenna.

Cast: **Edmund Lowe** as Chartrand, **Lois Moran** as Beverly Lane, **El Brendel** as Ole, **Howard Phillips** as Alexander, **Anders Van Haden** as a Police Officer.

Reviews: NY Times: 5 September 1931, p. 7; Variety: 8 September 1931, p. 15.

Some killer had the nerve to kill an audience member during stage magician Lowe's (Chartrand) act and now it's up to him to figure out who did it. Of course there is the skeptical police investigator who thinks Lowe is nuts, buts lets the magician stage a spooky séance which eventually reveals the killer.

The Motion Picture Guide.

Heartbreak
Fox - 8 November 1931.
Directed by Albert L. Werker.

Cast: **Charles Farrell** as John Merrick, **Madge Evans** as Countess Vilma Walden, **Paul Cavanagh** as Captain Wolke, **Anders Van Haden** - bit cast.

Reviews: NY Times: 17 October 1931, p. 20; Variety: 20 October 1931, p. 27.

A film set in Vienna in 1916 assures lots of waltzing, and this one delivers. Farrell is berated by his commanding officers when he travels over enemy lines to visit his girl. He brings her the unfortunate news that he killed her brother in an aerial battle, and tells her how sorry he is. She tosses him out, but changes her mind and calls him back--after all, he did risk his life to see her.

The Motion Picture Guide.

The Yellow Ticket
Fox - 15 November 1931.
Directed by Raoul Walsh.

Cast: **Lionel Barrymore** as Baron Igor Andrey, **Elissa Landi** as Marya Kalish, **Laurence Olivier** as Julian Rolfe, **Boris Karloff** as an Orderly, **Anders Van Haden** as a Police Officer.

Reviews: NY Times: 31 October 1931, p. 22; Variety: 3 November 1931, p. 27.

The Yellow Ticket

Landi, a Jewish girl, attempts to travel through her native Russia in 1913 to see her father which is dying in a St. Petersburg prison. The only way she can get permission to travel is with a "yellow ticket," which identifies her as a prostitute. In St. Petersburg she learns that her father has died, but while in the city, she falls in love with Olivier, a British Journalist. After hearing her story, he writes a number of articles for British and American newspaper that express the oppressed condition of the Russian people under the Czar's rule. When Barrymore, the chief of the Czar's secret police, becomes aware of Olivier's articles, he tries to imprison the scribe. Barrymore's primary objective, however, is to get Landi in bed, and when he tries, she kills him. As Austria invades the country, the lovers escape to England.

The Motion Picture Guide.

**Elissa Landi, unidentified guard, and Anders Van Haden.
(Photo from collection of Myra Van Haden).**

Ambassador Bill
Fox – 22 November 1931.
Directed by Sam Taylor.

Cast: **Will Rogers** as Bill Harper, **Marguerite Churchill** as Queen Vania, **Greta Nissen** as Countess Ilka, **Ray Milland** as King Lothar, **Anders Van Haden** as a Foreign Diplomat.

Reviews: NY Times: 14 November 1931, p. 15; Variety: 17 November 1931, p. 15.

Hokum about an Oklahoma cattleman, Rogers, who is appointed American ambassador to a country whose king has been exiled amid spasmodic revolutions by its inhabitants. Rogers saves the day with his rustic observations and home spun philosophy. For Will Rogers fans only.

The Motion Picture Guide.

Note: Anders' role appearance in this movie is one of the better roles that he has had as his conversation with Will Rogers presents an excellent example of his eloquent speech.

Anders Van Haden and Will Rogers. (Photo from collection of Myra Van Haden).

Surrender
Fox - 6 December 1931.
Directed and Produced by William K. Howard.

Cast: **Warner Baxter** as Sgt. Dumaine, **Leila Hyams** as Axelle, **Ralph Bellamy** as Capt. Ebling, **Anders Van Haden** - bit cast.

Reviews: NY Times: 28 November 1931, p. 20; Variety: 1 December 1931, p. 21.

Poorly made drama involving Baxter as a POW during WWI. He's a Frenchman being held in a German prison camp. Meanwhile, at a nearby castle a proud father dreams of the day his four sons will march into Paris for a great German victory. One son is engaged to Hyams, but she is trying to have an affair with Baxter. The drama is poorly written and often confusing, though Bellamy gives a good performance as a prison guard. Surrender is what cast and director did with this muddled story.

The Motion Picture Guide.

Good Sport
Fox - 13 December 1931.
Directed by Kenneth MacKenna.

Cast: **Linda Watkins** as Marilyn Parker, **John Boles** as Boyce Cameron, **Gretta Nissen** as Peggy Burns, **Hedda Hopper** as Mrs. Atherton, **Anders Van Haden** - bit cast.

Reviews: NY Times: 12 December 1931, p. 23.

The witty romantic drama takes a light view of prostitution, indicating that love, the type that makes one lose all self control, is not all that it's cracked up to be. This look into the realm of high-class ladies-of-the-night has a thin plot of a young married woman, Watkins, who discovers that her honorable husband has been carrying on some affairs on the side. In an attempt to try to get to the bottom this, Watkins winds up getting into a mess by having an extramarital affair of her own. Though the subject is a little risqué, it is kept low key, approached in a manner to emphasize the humor.

The Motion Picture Guide.

Delicious
Fox - 26 December 1931.
Directed by David Butler.

Cast: **Janet Gaynor** as Heather Gordon, **Charles Farrell** as Jerry Beaumont, **Paul Roulien** as Sascha, **Virginia Cherill** as Diana, **Anders Van Haden** as an Immigration Official.

Reviews: NY Times: 26 December 1931, p. 15; Variety: 29 December 1931, p. 166.

Gaynor plays a young Scottish lass on her way to America with her uncle in this overlong and disappointing Ira and George Gershwin musical celebrating immigration. While on board, Gaynor makes friends with a group of Russian musicians who have stowed away. One of them, Roulien, falls in love with her and writes her a song. But Gaynor falls for rich polo-player Farrell who spends most of the rest of the movie dumping his pretty and boring fiancée Cherill and seeing the lovely Scottish girl as his true love. Songs include: "Somebody From Somewhere" (sung by Gaynor), "Delishious" (Roulien), "Blah-Blah-Blah" (Brandel); "We're From The Journal, The Wahrheit, The Telegram, The Times"; "Katinkitschka" (Gaynor), and "The New York Rhapsody."

The Motion Picture Guide.

Anders Van Haden and Janet Gaynor. (Photo from collection of Myra Van Haden).

Charlie Chan's Chance
Fox - 24 January 1932.
Directed by John G. Blystone and Produced by Joseph August.

Cast: **Warner Oland** as Charlie Chan, **H. B. Warner** as Inspector Fife, **Marion Nixon** as Shirley Marlowe, **James Kirkwood** as Inspector Flannery, **Ralph Morgan** as Barry Kirk, **James Todd** as Kenneth Dunwood, **Anders Van Haden** - bit cast.

Reviews: NY Times: 23 January 1932, p. 18; Variety: 26 January 1932, p. 23.

Scotland Yard and New York sleuths are no match for Charlie as he outwits master mind Todd, despite countless false clues. Technical detail is excellent, especially in a studio version of the East River at night which provides brilliance. This time Chan himself is the intended murder victim, avoiding death only by chance while another is killed instead and he must solve this killing through inventive sleuthing. Oland renders the traditional epigrams and sage-like lines such as "Some heads, like nuts, much better if well cracked." (This film has been reported to be one of four Charlie Chan films that are lost.)

The Motion Picture Guide.

While Paris Sleeps
Fox - 8 May 1932.
Directed by Alan Dwan and Produced by William Sistrom.

Cast: **Victor McLaglen** as Jacques Costaud, **Helen Mack** as Mannon Costaud, **William Bakewell** as Paul Renoir, **Anders Van Haden** - bit cast.

Reviews: Variety: 14 June 1932, p. 17.

Effectively stark depiction of the white slave trade in Paris has McLaglen as an escaped convict journeying to the City of Lights to try to save his daughter from the clutches of lecherous pimps. One of the more striking scenes has the hoods taking care of an informant by sticking him into the burning oven of the bakery that serves as the front for their corrupt dealings.

The Motion Picture Guide.

Anders Van Haden and Victor Mc Laglen.
(Photo from the of collection of Constance J. Hurt).

Cheaters at Play
Fox - 14 February 1932.
Directed by Hamilton McFadden.

Cast: **Thomas Meighan** as Michael Lanyard, **Charlotte Greenwood** as Mrs. Crozier, **Anders Van Haden** as the Captain.

Reviews: NY Times: 27 February 1932, p. 22; Variety: 1 March 1932, p. 21.

Shipboard caper has reformed jewel thief tracking down #375,000 in stolen pearls while at the same time trying to teach a long-lost son to live the legitimate life. But it's too late for the kid, who made his mind up ago to go into dad's business. Too many incongruities make this an incoherent film, including one odd scene wherein the crooks are morse-coding each other by tapping on bridge tables or spelling out supposedly subtle messages by a smoking pipe on teeth. Poorly directed.

The Motion Picture Guide.

Charlotte Greenwood, unidentified, Anders Van Haden, and Thomas Meighan. (Photo from collection of Myra Van Haden).

Cheaters at Play

Thomas Meighan and Anders Van Haden. (Photo
from collection of Myra Van Haden).

Rasputin and the Empress
MGM - 24 March 1932.
Directed by Richard Boleslavsky and Charles J. Brabin. Produced by Bernard Hyman.

Cast: **Ethel Barrymore** as Empress Alexandra, **John Barrymore** as Prince Paul Chegodieff, **Lionel Barrymore** as Rasputin, **Diana Wynyard** as Natasha, Ralph Morgan as Emperor Nikolai, Tad Alexander as Alexis, Gustov von Seyffertitz as Dr. Wolfe, **Mischa Auer** as the Butler, **Anders Van Haden** as the Major-Domo.

Reviews: NY Times: 24 December 1932, p. 11; Variety: 27 December 19, p. 14.

The role of the majordomo that Anders plays in this video is brief and you hear his voice before you see him announcing visiting dignitaries to the court.

Anders Van Haden in front as the Major-Domo.
(Photograph from the collection of Myra Van Haden).

A Passport to Hell
Fox - 14 August 1932.
Directed by Frank Lloyd.

Cast: **Elissa Landi** as Myra Carson, **Paul Lukas** as Lt. Kurt Kurtoff, **Warner Oland** as Baron von Sydow, **Donald Crisp** as Sgt. Snyder, **Anders Van Haden** as an Immigration Officer.

Reviews: NY Times: 27 August 1932, p. 13; Variety: 30 August 1932, p. 21.

A dull melodrama starring Landi, who is deported to Germany after being blamed for a man's suicide. WWI breaks and the woman marries the son of a German commandant to avoid being put into an alien prison camp. She has an affair with another officer, while her husband sells secrets to the English to pay for Landi to leave the country. He commits suicide, but Landi rips up the confession note to save his honor. She leaves the country in hopes of seeing her lover once the war is over. Features Oland taking a break from his "Charlie Chan" series to play the commandant.

The Motion Picture Guide.

Unidentified, Anders Van Haden as an Immigration Officer, Unidentified.
(Photograph from the collection of Myra Van Haden).

The Fighting Marshall

Columbia - 18 December 1931.
Directed by D. Ross Lederman.

Cast: **Tim McCoy** as Tim Benton, **Dorothy Gulliver** as Alice Wheeler, **Mathew Betz** as Red Larkin, **Mary Carr** as Aunt Emily, **W. A. Howell** as Marshall Bob Dinsmore.

Reviews: Variety: 12 April 1932, p. 15.

A fairly new wrinkle for a western - this having the hero start as an escaped convict and wind up in the clothes of a new but dead marshall. Tim McCoy has the role. Even though there is a consequent theme song in an artificial background and a lot of fisticuffs that provoke some laughs. "The Fighting Marshal" is tried a true material that always satisfies in lesser grinds.

There is a plot within a plot and villains abundant. Naturally McCoy was railroaded, and, just as naturally, the two men who did the deed are living happily in the town in which Tim decides to do the marshall masquerade.

Variety.

Anders Van Haden, credited in this film as W. A. Howell, aka William A. Howell, has a good role in this "B" Western. He jumps down from the attic and surprises Tim McCoy and Mathew Betz and identifies himself as Marshall Bob Dinsmore. Mathew Betz, the nasty convict Red Larkin, eventually overpowers and kills the marshall.

Mathew Betz, William A. Howell, Tim McCoy.
(Photograph from the collection of Myra Van Haden).

The Jungle Mystery
Universal - 5 August to 2 November 1932.
A 12 Episode Serial Directed by Ray Taylor.

Into the Dark Continent	The Jaws of Death	The Ivory Trail
Trapped by the Enemy	The Death Stream	The Jungle Terror
Poisoned Fangs	Ambushed	The Mystery Cavern
The Lion's Fury	Daylight Doom	Buried Treasure

Cast: **Tom Tyler** as Kirk Montgomery, **Cecilia Parker** as Barbara Morgan, **Philo McCullough** as Shillow, **Noah Berry, Jr.** as Fred Oakes, **Sam Baker** as Zunga, **Anders Van Haden**.

While hunting in Africa, Tyler and his friend Berry encounter Philo McCullough, a rival hunter, who is searching for a vast store of Ivory. Kirk and Fred later meet Cecilia and her father who are seeking the girl's missing brother. The two friends decide to team up with the Morgans and aid them in their quest. Shillow and his gang, which includes the treacherous adventuress Belle Waldron, do their best to obstruct and discourage the Morgan party, fearing that the latter group is also after the ivory. Shillow's schemes are aided when the friends encounter wild beasts and unfriendly natives, and get entangled in a series of captures and escapes. The friends are helped by a mysterious jungle ape-man named Zungu who has a sympathetic disposition toward virtues as well as a split-second sense of timing. With his help, the friends soon rout the Shillow party, and find Barbara's brother. Tom and Cecelia can look forward to a more relaxed relationship.

To Be Continued...

Cast of The Ivory Trail - Center trio: Frank Lacteen,
Tom Tyler, Ray Taylor with Cecilia Parker
below, Noah Berry, Jr. Philo McCullough, and Anders Van Haden at the far right.
(Hollywood Museum Collection, Courtesy of the
Academy of Motion Picture Arts and Sciences).

The Jungle Mystery

Cast still of Anders Van Haden from The Jungle Mystery.
(Photograph from the collection of Myra Van Haden).

The Match King
Warner's First National – 31 December 1932.
Directed by Howard Bretherton and Produced by Hal Willis.

Cast: **Warren William** as Paul Kroll, **Lili Damita** as Marta Molnar, **Glenda Farrell** as Babe, **Anders Van Haden** – bit cast.

Reviews: NY Times: 8 December 1932, p. 25; Variety: 13 December 1932, p. 15.

This is an unabashed biography of one of the most spectacular world-wide swindlers of all time, Ivar Kreuger, made hot on the heels of Kreuger's suicide in Paris after he was exposed as giant fraud, having bilked tens of thousands of investors out of countless millions by selling worthless stock in his many bogus European companies. The film begins in Paris as William, playing Kroll/Kreuger, realizes he is about to be revealed as a swindler and contemplates suicide. He thinks back to his earliest beginnings and in flashback, he is shown as a street sweeper in Chicago, where he plans a murder in his fantastic scheme to monopolize something used repeatedly every day, the common kitchen match. He swindles banker into pumping lots of money into his phony firms, using and discarding women along the way as if they were burned-out matches. On his rise to ill-gotten riches, the suave William attacks a famous European film star, played by Damita, who dresses, acts, and talks like Greta Garbo, and for good reason. Garbo was one of Kreuger's real-life victims, reportedly duped into investing substantial funds in his bogus schemes. The film comes very close to reality, even detailing the method by which William/Kreuger negotiated a $40 million loan from Wall Street financiers (which actually happened). Director Bretherton deftly, and with startling pace, details a sinister career of murder, blackmail, and forgery that is no less fanciful than Kreuger's actual machinations. (Kreuger built his fortune by offering some Italian bonds, which he had masterfully forged, as collateral for his multimillion dollar loans and only when these bonds were determined to be fake did his career end.) The overall production of this film is superior and William is a wonder to behold as he handles his conniving role with marvelous restraint. Damita is a bit campy as the Garbo-like actress who dumps her lover-entrepreneur after suspecting his empire is about to collapse. All in all, THE MATCH KING is an intriguing artifact of the early talkie era.

The Motion Picture Guide.

Cavalcade
Fox - 15April 1933.
Directed by Frank Lloyd and Produced by Winfield Sheehan.
Academy Award - Best Picture of the Year.

Cast: **Diana Wynyard** as Jane Marryot, **Clive Brook** as Robert Marryot, **Una O'Conner** as Ellen Bridges, **Anders Van Haden** - bit cast.

Reviews: NY Times: 6 January 1933, p. 23; Variety: 18 July 1933, p. 37.

Noel Coward, in one of his serious ventures, traces thirty tears of a British family's life from the Boer War through WWI and into the Jazz Age. A big fine production little shown or remembered today; CAVALCADE was a sensation at the time of its movie release, filled as it is with a wistful look at a couple clinging together through years of love. The epochal scenes start with the Boer War and go on to record the death of Queen Victoria, WWI, the sinking of the Titanic, and the birth of jazz. Though strictly a British film, it was done so well that it won an Oscar for the best film of 1933. It also was one of the earliest movies of child movie star Bonita Granville.

The Motion Picture Guide.

The Great Jasper
RKO - 3 March 1933.
Directed by J. Walter Ruben and Produced
by Kenneth MacGowan.

Cast: **Richard Dix** as Jasper Horn, **Wera Engels** as Norma McGowd, **Edna May Oliver** as Madame Talma, **Anders Van Haden** as a Conductor.

Reviews: NY Times: 17 February 1933, p. 15; Variety: 21 February 1933, p. 14.

Dix is an Irish Don Juan who gets into a lot of trouble because of his amorous tendencies. A motorman at the turn of the century, he is loyal to his wife, only in that he doesn't run away with any of the many women he makes love to. We see him changing jobs and women, until finally he retires in Atlantic City as a somewhat moralistic reader of women's fortunes, and dies after doing some good.

The Motion Picture Guide.

Anders has small role, saying only two lines, in this film during a scene inside the trolley barn prior to the departure of the first electric trolley.

Anders Van Haden, Richard Dix, unidentified. (Photo from collection of Myra Van Haden).

Secret of the Blue Room

Universal - 20 July 1933.
Directed by Kurt Neumann and Produced by Carl Maemmle, Jr.

Cast: **Gloria Stuart** as Irene von Hellsdorf, **Paul Lukas** as Capt. Walter Brink, **Lionel Atwill** as Robert von Hellsdorf, **Onslow Stevens** as Frank Faber, **William Janney** as Thomas Brandt, Edward **Arnold** as the Police Commissioner, **Anders Van Haden** as The Stranger [appears in the credits].

Reviews: NY Times: 13 September 1933, p. 22; Variety: 19 September 1933, p. 13.

A good haunted house mystery starring Stuart as a strange woman who forces her three suitors Janney, Stevens, and Lukas, to prove their bravery by each spending a night alone in the mysterious blue room of an old castle owned by Atwill, where three people were murdered twenty years before. Remade twice, as THE MISSING GUEST (1938) and again as MURDER IN THE BLUE ROOM (1944).

The Motion Picture Guide.

Anders Van Haden in the center with the flashlight beam on shining on his face.
(Photo courtesy of the Pentagram Library collection).

Reunion in Vienna
MGM - 16 June 1933.
Directed by Sidney Franklin.

Cast: **John Barrymore** as Archduke Rudolf Von Habsburg, **Diana Wynyard** as Elena Krug, **Frank Morgan** as Dr. Anton Krug, **Henry Travers** as Father Krug, **Una Merkel** as Ilsa Hinnrich, **Anders Van Haden** as an Aristocrat.

Reviews: NY Times: 29 April 1933.

John Barrymore is perfectly cast as the fallen Habsburg prince, Rudolf, reduced to making a living as a taxicab driver by the fortunes of war and the fall of the empire. Barrymore brings to this role the perfect mix of tragedy, bathos, and comic self-deprecation. Diana Wynyard is entirely believable as his erstwhile lover dissatisfied with the clinical attentions of her psychiatrist husband, Frank Morgan, and longing for the lost days at Schoenbrun. Eduardo Cianelli, Henry Travers, Una Merkle, and May Robson round out the ensemble cast in this highly enjoyable period piece. Sadly, as Diana Wynyard's character finds, we all have to live in the present.

Silent's Fan.

Best of Enemies
Fox- 23 June 1933.
Directed by Rian James.

Cast: **Buddy Rodgers** as Jimmie Hartman, **Frank Morgan** as William Hartman, **Marion Nixon** as Lena Schneider, **Joseph Cawthorn** as Gus Schneider, **Greta Nissen** as The Blonde, **Anders Van Haden** as Professor Herman.

Reviews: NY Times: 17 July 1933, p. 19; Variety: 18 July 1933, p. 37.

Conflict between Cawthorn and Morgan is tempered when the son and daughter of each of the arch-enemies meet and fall in love. Producer went through three directors, thereby diluting the film's impact.

The Motion Picture Guide.

Madame Spy
Universal - 28 January 1934.
Directed by Karl Freund and Produced by Carl Maemmle, Jr.

Cast: **Fay Wray** as Maria, **Edward Arnold** as Schultz, **Nils Asther** as Capt. Franck, **Noah Berry** as General Philipow, **Anders Van Haden** as a Detective.

Reviews: NY Times: 10 February 1934, p. 20; Variety: 13 February 1934, p. 14.

Totally implausible but beautifully shot film directed by former cameraman Karl Freund, in which German captain Asther is hired by the Austrian secret service to capture a mysterious Russian agent known only as B-24. Unfortunately, agent B-24 happens to be Asther's own very Russian (well as Russian as Fay Wray could get) wife. Remade from a German film entitled UNDER FALSE FLAGS (1932).

The Motion Picture Guide.

Snug in the Jug
RKO Short - 24 November 1934.
Directed by Ben Holmes and Produced by Lou Brock.

Cast: **Bobby Clark** as Dr. Peri Winkle, **Paul McCullough** as Major Blodgett, **Harry Gribbon** as Slug Mullen, **Anders Van Haden** as Herr Professor Eisenkopf, **Russell Powell** as the Warden?, **Lelia Leslie** as Mrs. Van Ryder, **James Morton** as the butler?, **Harry Bowen** as the Commodore?

Reviews: Variety: 27 January 1933, p. 17.

Clark and McCullogh hit the lowest strain of meaningless non-sense in 'Snug in a Jug.' It's just a lot of aimless filler. The crew must have been unusually weary when they ploughed through this hit or miss. There are gags older than some of the hills. The would-be travesty has the boys being discharged from a jail, where, according to inferences, the warden is, or would like to be, a nance. Then there's a tough mugg at liberty. About the only idea the young thing conveys is plastering of the town with reward signs.

C&M don't have to try for silliness in this because everything about it is forced. And a sprinkling of CN over some of the gags might not be a bad idea. Anders' role as Herr Professor Eisenkopf is fairly important in this short. He is a criminologist who trying to catch the elusive thief Slug Mullen.

Variety.

Anders Van Haden as Herr Professor Eisenhopf.
(Photo from collection of Myra Van Haden).

Riptide
MGM - 30 March 1934.
Directed by Edmund Goulding and
Produced by Irving Thalberg.

Cast: **Norma Shearer** as Lady Mary Rexford, **Robert Montgomery** as Tommie Trent, **Herbert Marshall** as Lord Philip Rexford, **Anders Van Haden** as a German Porter.

Reviews: NY Times: 31 March 1934, p. 8; Variety: 3 April 1934, p. 17.

Shearer plays a carefree American who has a child after an affair with Marshall, an English lord. The two marry and their future seems blissful. Marshall goes off on a business trip to America, leaving his wife behind with nothing to do. Shearer is soon bored and attends a swanky party where she bumps into an old flame, Montgomery. At one time Montgomery's playboy personality had quelled any hopes of marriage between the two but their reunion fires up some old passions. He makes an unsuccessful pass at Shearer, then follows her home in a drunken stupor. Montgomery climbs up Shearer's terrace in his efforts to renew his love and ends up taking a bad fall. He is taken to the hospital which results in some scandalous press for both Montgomery and Shearer. When Marshall returns home he is incensed at the accounts of his wife's would-be affair. Though Shearer tries to explain what really happened. Marshall refuses to listen. Convinced his wife has been dallying with Montgomery behind his back, Marshall decides to separate from Shearer. This leaves her free to pursue other men and she quickly finds herself in Montgomery's arms. Marshall comes to his senses and tries to win back his wife but upon discovering she has been secretly carrying on with Montgomery, he goes ahead with the divorce proceedings. Before the legal work is completed, however, Marshall and Shearer realize how much they really do love each other and decide to remain together after all.

The Motion Picture Guide.

Note: Anders' off-camera role is really that of a German speaking Swiss Porter who is only heard when Marshall and Shearer are at a Saint Moritz hotel.

Little Man, What Now?
Universal - 4 June 1934.
Directed by Franz Borzage and Produced by Carl Laemmle, Jr.

Cast: **Margaret Sullivan** as Emma Merceau, **Douglass Montogomery** as Hans Pinneberg, **Hedda Hopper** as a Nurse, **Anders Van Haden** as a Soap Box Orator.

Reviews: NY Times: 1 June 1934, p. 29; Variety: 5 June 1934, p. 12.

After the news of their secret marriage leaks out, newlyweds Sullivan and Montgomery leave their small town for pre-Hitler Berlin. They live with Doucet, the groom's stepmother, in what turns out to be a well-disguised, high-class bordello. Montgomery quits his meager department store job and they pack their bags. Enroute to nowhere in particular, they stay in a loft owned by an old wagon driver, where Sullivan gives birth to a son (the "little man" of the title). Soon thereafter, Montgomery is offered a job in Holland, leaving Germany just as the Weimar Republic is about to fall. One of the finest films of the 1930s to deal with Germany's political and social crisis, and a wonderful romance from Borage.

The Motion Picture Guide.

Note: In the beginning scenes of this movie, Anders Van Haden appears as an orator atop a soap box and speaks a few lines.

Stamboul Quest
MGM - 17 July 1934.
Directed by Sam C. Wood and Produced
by Bernard H. Hyman.

Cast: **Myrna Loy** as Annemarie, **George Brent** as Beall, **Lionel Atwill** as Von Strum, **C. Henry Gordon** as Ali Bey, **Anders Van Haden** as a Conductor.

Reviews: NY Times: 14 July 1934, p. 16; Variety: 17 July 1934, p. 15.

Loy was appearing in her first solo starring role in this unfortunately titled movie that was much better than the business it did. She was playing a German heroine, which was unusual at the time, because WWI was fresh in the memory and there was already a rumbling from behind the German border that would presage the establishment of the Third Reich. Loy essays the part of a real woman who was known as "Fraulein Doktor" and who, it is said was the person who ordered the death of the redoubtable Mata Hari when she learned that the other female spy had fallen in love. There is no room for sentiment in the spying business. It's 1915 and the chief of operations for the Kaiser's intelligence office is Atwill, a no-nonsense pedant who is worried that information about is country's military operations in the Dardanelles is being discovered by the Allies. In order to stem the flow of data, he sends his top operative, Loy, to Turkey. The No. 1 suspect is Gordon, who runs the Turkish military units and they think that he might be trading the information for money. While in Berlin, Loy meets American med student Brent and he falls head over heels for her, never knowing that she is an undercover agent. When she goes off to Constantinople, Brent chases after her like a young swain in love, and Loy has to keep him at arm's length in order to get her work done. She manages to solve the puzzle and then Atwill tells her that Brent has been shot for being in the wrong place at the wrong time. By now she's fallen in love with him and the news of his death sends her over the edge and she repairs to a monastery to regain her mental health. But Atwill has been lying, and when Brent finds her, they are united. Sounds melodramatic but Mankiewicz's script sparkles with sharp insights and the nature of the assertive woman and the Naive man is a switch on many other situations that plays well.

The Motion Picture Guide.

Lionell Atwell as Von Strum, Anders Van Haden as the conductor. (Photo from collection of Myra Van Haden).

The World Moves On
Fox - 31 August 1934.
Directed by John Ford and Produced by Winfield R. Sheehan.

Cast: **Madeleine Carroll** as Mary Warburton, **Franchot Tone** as Richard Giraud, **Anders Van Haden** as a German Doctor.

Reviews: NY Times: 30 June 1934, p. 18; Variety: 3 July 1934, p. 26.

A will read in the 1800s links the fortunes of two prominent New Orleans families represented by Carroll and Tone. Their wealth grows, leading to expansion in both France and Germany, but WW I and the market plunge of the 1920s destroy the families' empire. However, Carroll and Tone survive the debacle and begin anew. A strong anti-war statement, this includes some striking battle footage culled from an earlier French feature, CROSSES OF WOOD. Dramatic war scenes of this sort would become a staple of John Ford's latter films. THE WORLD MOVES ON also included the first performance by Carroll in a U.S. production.

The Motion Picture Guide.

Love Time
Fox - 21 September 1934.
Directed by James Tinling and Produced by John Stone.

Cast: **Pat Paterson** as Valerie, **Nils Asther** as Franz Schubert, **Henry B. Walthall** as Duke Johann von Hatzfeld, **Hermin Bing** as Istvan, **Anders Van Haden** as 2nd Policeman.

Reviews: Variety: 6 November 1934, p. 17.

Romanticized version of the love life of composer Franz Schubert. Paterson plays the daughter of a Duke exiled by the Emperor because of her mother's marriage. She tries to make plans for an elopement with the composer, Asther, but he flees because he does not want to ruin Paterson's life. But the girl never gives up in her pursuit of the composer. The story is thin, with an attempt to pad it with unneeded dramatics and misplaced comic relief. The direction is uneven, with Paterson poorly cast. The rest of the performances are good, but wasted.

The Motion Picture Guide.

We Live Again
Goldwyn/UA - 16 November 1934.
Directed by Rouben Mamoulian and
Produced by Samuel Goldwyn.

Cast: **Anna Sten** as Katusha Maslava, **Frederic March** as Prince Dmitri Nekhlyudov, **Jane Baxter** as Missy Kortchagin, **C. Aubrey Smith** as Prince Kortchagin, **Anders Van Haden** as a Russian General.

Reviews: NY Times: 2 November 1934, p. 27; Variety: 6 November 1934, p. 16.

This fine adaptation of Tolstoy's oft-filmed novel RESURRECTION opens in the countryside of Czarist Russia where a prince (March) grows up with Sten, a peasant servant girl. The two feel like social equals and Sten falls in love with the dashing March. He goes into the service and returns after two years to find Sten's affection unchanged. Seven years pass and March (now with a beard) is engaged to marry Baxter, daughter of a fellow Russian prince, Smith. Smith invites March to sit in as a juror on a murder case he is trying, involving a prostitute charged with murder. Sten is found guilty and sentenced to exile in Siberia. March tries to get Sten released, but she only mocks her former lover's efforts. March decides he must pay for the suffering he has caused Sten, and consequently gives up all his land to his retainers. This classic story of redemption is beautifully told under Mamoulian's strong direction. March and Sten are excellent as the tragic lovers, giving their roles depth and intensity.

The Motion Picture Guide.

Anders Van Haden as the Russian General.
(Photo from collection of William D. Howard & Myra Van Haden).

The County Chairman
Fox - 11 January 1935.
Directed by John Blystone and Produced
by Edward W. Butcher.

Cast: **Will Rogers** as Jim Hackler, **Evelyn Venable** as Lucy Rigby, **Kent Taylor** as Ben Jarvey, **Mickey Rooney** as Freckles, **Berton Churchill** as Elias Rigby, **Anders Van Haden** as Man in Bowling Alley.

Reviews: Variety: 22 January 1935, p. 14.

A story of small time politics in 1880s Wyoming has Rogers as the attorney who promotes his adopted son, Taylor, in a race for public prosecutor against corrupt incumbent Churchill. Starts out slow but not bad once it gets going, and for an appearance that suits the personality, talents, and voice of the legendary Rogers this should not be missed.

The Motion Picture Guide.

Mystery Woman
Fox - 15 January 1935.
Directed by Eugene Ford and Produced by John Stone.

Cast: **Mona Barrie** as Margaret Benoit, **Gilbert Roland** as Juan Santanda, **John Holliday** as Dr. **Theodore Van Wyke**, Rod LaRocque as Jacques Benoit, **Anders Van Haden** as a Commander.

Reviews: NY Times: 9 January 1935, p. 22; Variety: 22 January 1935, p. 14.

LeRocque has been wrongly sent to Devil's Island. His freedom depends on a document that proves he is innocent of treason. The chase is on between enemies Roland, Halliday, and LaRocque's wife, Barrie, on who will get the important paper. The usual intrigues and murders occur but as expected, Barrie winds up freeing her husband. The cat-and-mouse game between the three principals is interesting at first but quickly wears down under the uninspired direction and weak dialog.

The Motion Picture Guide.

The Florentine Dagger
Warner Bros. – 30 March 1935.
Directed by Robert Florey and Produced by Harry Joe Brown.

Cast: **Donald Woods** as Juan Cesare, **Margaret Lindsay** as Florence Ballau, **C. Aubrey Smith** as Dr. Lytton, **Anders Van Haden** as a Bidder.

Reviews: NY Times: 27 April 1935, p. 20; Variety: 1 May 1935, p. 17.
Woods is a descendant of the renaissance Borgias. After visiting his ancestral castle in Italy, he becomes a successful playwright but also come to believe that he has inherent killer instincts. Enter Lindsay, whom Woods selects to play the femme fatale in his new hit play, believing her to be another Lucretia Borgia. A murder occurs and Woods, Lindsay, and even the psychiatrist, Smith, treating Woods are equal suspects. The Ben Hecht novel upon which this film is based is better than the movie, one where the author detailed three suspects with dual personalities, a theme not fully developed in the film. Woods and Lindsay are fine, and Smith, that venerable British character actor, brightens every scene he plays. Florey directs with lightning speed, as was his special trait.

The Motion Picture Guide.

Folies Bergère de Paris
Fox - 22 February 1935.
Directed by Roy Del Ruth and Produced by Darryl F. Zanuck.

Cast: **Maurice Chevalier** as Eugene Charlier/Fernand, the Baron Cassini, **Merle Oberon** as Baroness Genevieve Cassini, **Ann Sothern** as Mimi, **Anders Van Haden** as a Principal in Montage.

Reviews: NY Times: 25 February, p. 13; Variety: 27 February 1935, p. 12.

This is one of those rare films that was filmed simultaneously in two languages by the same director. Chevalier plays the role in both films, but in the French version, L'HOMME DES FOLIES BERGERE, Natalie Paley was Baroness Cassini and Mimi was played by Sim Viva. The plot was a duplicate in both, with Chevalier in two roles. In the first part, he is a wealthy Baron whose fortune is at risk, requiring him to be in two places at once. He's supposed to attend a fancy dress ball as well as a secret meeting about his finances. His partners decide to hire a Folies Bergére performer who is known for his eerie imitations of people, one of whom is the famous Baron. He has only to play the part for the duration of the gala ball and no one tells the Baron's wife, Oberon. Chevalier, as the entertainer, is attentive to his "wife" but she rebuffs him (they are separated at the time). Then he learns that the Baron has been romancing his stage partner, Sothern. The next day, the Baron is not to be found so the performer must again impersonate him. While posing as the Baron he tells Sothern that their affair can no longer go on. At first, Sothern is disappointed, then realizes that she loves the entertainer, not Baron. Meanwhile, the Baron has engineered a financial deal that garners him a huge amount of francs. Oberon is much more attentive to him than usual, which he likes. What he doesn't like is that Sothern now swears her affection to the Baron's look-alike. The Baron finally understands that Oberon is the woman for him but is annoyed by the knowledge that she is back in his arms as the result of the impersonator's efforts and he is forever to wonder how far Oberon went with the charlatan. Worse, he'll never know if she knew that it wasn't him for the past two days.

The Motion Picture Guide.

Note: Anders' appearance is only for a brief glimpse towards the end of the movie in Chevalier's closing musical number.

Les Misérables
20th Century - 21 April 1935.
Directed by Richard Bolenslawski and
Produced by Darryl F. Zanuck.

Cast: **Fredric March** as Jean Valjean/Champmatheu, **Charles Laughton** as Emile Javert, **Sir Cedric Hardwicke** as Bishop Bienvenue, **Frances Drake** as Eponine, **John Beal** as Marius, **Florence Eldridge** as Fantine, **William P. Carelton** as the 1st Judge in Arras, **Anders Van Haden** as the 2nd Judge in Arras.

Reviews: NY Times: 21 April 1935, p. 14; Variety: 24 April 1934, p. 12.

Note: The role of that of the 2nd Judge in Arras is portrayed excellently by Anders Van Haden in the court room scene in Arras.

**William P. Carelton in center with Anders Van Haden on the right.
(Photograph from the collection of Myra Van Haden).**

Les Misérables

March is overwhelming as the sensitive, persecuted Jean Valjean who steals a loaf of bread to survive, is captured, and given 10 years at hard labor in prison. When finally escaping the prison galley, March is a hard-bitten, stone-hearted, and utterly unsympathetic creature whose compassion for his fellow has been hammered out of him by the cruelty of confinement. He is taken by Hardwicke, a Bishop who refuses to prosecute him for stealing two silver candlesticks, and, through Hardwicke's kindness and understanding, March regains his sensitivity, totally reforming. He works night and day to build a new life for himself using another name, taking a young child as his own. He becomes a well-to-do businessman and moving to another town, becomes so widely liked that he is elected mayor. His grown daughter, Drake, and he live in a resplendent house and every waking day of March's life is devoted to benefiting his fellow man. His chief of police, Laughton, is less than convivial, however. He is a police bloodhound, one of those cold, unimpassioned officials, who knows no humanity, only the letter of the law. To the single-minded Laughton the law is to be upheld and enforced at all costs, with no mercy shown to anyone causing the slightest infraction. Laughton and March clash repeatedly over the interpretation of the law and the policeman becomes incensed when March intercedes on behalf of social pariah, Eldridge (March's real-life wife). One day March sees a villager trapped beneath a heavy wagon and, with what seems to be superhuman strength, he puts his back to the wagon and lifts it so the man can be saved. Laughton watches this feat and is reminded of a galley prisoner he once encountered. He begins to investigate March's past and identifies March as Jean Valjean, the wanted criminal. He is then confused when another prisoner is found, a mindless inmate who amazingly resembles March, and who admits he is Jean Valjean. He is put on trial but the honest-to-the-bone March (who plays both parts) admits he is the real Jean Valjean. Before he can be jailed he again escapes with Drake to Paris where he assumes yet another identity. His daughter falls in love with Beal, a young radical who works for prison reform. Laughton arrives in Paris and is assigned to watch the revolutionaries. He gets onto March's trail once more as March becomes more and more involved with Beal and his revolutionary friends. Half of Paris revolts against inhuman conditions and Drake suddenly runs to her father with the news that her love Beal has been injured in the fighting.

March goes to the barricades and finds the young man, carrying him to safety, but Laughton is right behind him. March escapes into the Paris sewers, carrying Beal through the treacherous chest-high waters until depositing him with his daughter. When he realizes that his daughter and Beal will be safe to lead a happy life together, March goes to surrender to Laughton. But the dogged policeman, who has witnessed March's selfless sacrifice, finds compassion stirring in his heart, an emotion he cannot understand and one that so confuses and vexes him that he is willing to break the law, the very fibre of his being, and allow the noble March his freedom. But he cannot do either. Laughton solves his traumatic dilemma by hurling himself into the Seine and drowning himself. March is free to rejoin his daughter and Beal, living out his life among those who love him. This full scale production is meticulous in every detail and faithful to the Hugo novel, except for allowing March to live in the end where he dies in the original tale. Boleslawski, a largely forgotten director today, was truly masterful in his handling of LES MISÉRABLES, adhering faithfully to Hugo's scenes.

The Motion Picture Guide.

The Bride of Frankenstein
Universal - 22 April 1935.
Directed by James Whale and Produced by Carl Laemmle.

Cast: **Boris Karloff** as The Monster, Frankenstein; **Colin Clive** as Henry Frankenstein, **Valerie Hobson** as Elizabeth Frankenstein, **Elsa Lanchester** as Mary Wollstonecraft Shelley and The Monster's Mate; **O. P. Heggie** as The Hermit, **Ernest Thesiger** as Dr. Septimus Pretorious, **Gavin Gordon** as Lord Byron, **Douglas Walton** as Percy Shelley, **Dwight Frye** as Karl, **Anne Darling** as The Shepherdess, **E. E. Clive** as the Burgomaster, **Walter Brennan** as the Neighbor, **Anders Van Haden** as a Villager.

Reviews: NY Times: 11 May 1935, p. 21; Variety: 15 May 1935, p. 19.

Note: A very brief role is played by Anders in this video as he appears as a villager outside the Burgomaster's house.

Anders Van Haden at the upper right.
(Photograph from the collection of Myra Van Haden).

The Daring Young Man
Fox - 24 May 1935.
Directed by William A. Seiter and Robert Kane.

Cast: **James Dunn** as Don McLane, **Mae Clarke** as Martha Allen, **Neil Hamilton** as Gerald Raeburn, **Anders Van Haden** as the Druggist.

Reviews: NY Times: 18 July 1935, p. 15; Variety: 24 July 1935, p. 56.

Dunn and Clarke are reporters for rival newspapers. Though they seem not to like each other at first, it is not too long before they fall in love. They are about to be married when Dunn gets shipped off to do an undercover story in prison, leaving Clarke standing at the altar. Perhaps the real story would have been to tell how a society writer like Dunn suddenly gets sent to do a hard crime story in prison.

The Motion Picture Guide.

James Dunn and Anders Van Haden.
(Photo from the collection of Constance J. Hurt,
daughter of Myra Van Haden).

Diamond Jim
Universal - 2 September 1935.
Directed by A. Edward Sutherland and
Produced by Edmund Grainger.

Cast: **Edward Arnold** as "Diamond Jim" James Buchanan Brady, **Jean Arthur** as Jane Mathews, **Binnie Barnes** as Lllian Russell, **Cesar Romero** as Jerry Richardson, **Anders Van Haden** - Bit Cast.

Reviews: NY Times: 24 August 1935, p. 18; Variety: 28 August 1935, p. 12.

The combination of a great subject and a great character actor should have produced a minor masterpiece but DIAMOND JIM misses the mark. Arnold, a golden-tongued thespian who never gave a bad performance, plays the title role with élan, beginning as a baggage man for the railroads, then a salesman, then a supplier of train equipment to every railroad in the nation. (Actually Diamond Jim made his fortune on the sale of barbed wire first, then railroad equipment.) Only about fifteen minutes is spent on chronicling Diamond Jim's rise when most of the movie should have been given over to this colorful career. The script and director Sutherland, who was always more at home with comedy, introduce several love themes that simply don't work, or, at least, they don't work for Arnold. He proposes early to hometown girl Arthur and she rejects him for another man; in fact, following his humble proposal, Arthur cold-bloodedly replies by asking him if he would like to attend her wedding to another. Arnold goes off to make his fortune and falls in love with Arthur's spitting image, which is logical because it's Arthur again in another role. Again she is having nothing to do with gracious, kind-hearted, open-pockets Arnold. She's in love with Romero. Arnold woos Barnes, who plays the famous Lllian Russell, but doesn't want him either. She's also in love with Romero. And Romero is busy spurning both ladies as he makes his playboy rounds. The rejection is simply too much for Arnold. A man with a bad stomach-his doctors have warned him to lay off the munchies-he decides to commit suicide by eating himself to death (shades of George Arliss in OLD ENGLISH). It is true that Brady embraced gluttony with both hands and the great quantity of rich foods he consumed contributed to his death in 1917 but the manner in which Arnold meets his fate over Barnes is ludicrous at best. Arnold nevertheless gives a bravura performance and he glitters like the walking Christmas Tree that was Diamond Jim Brady, expansive, awarding wonderful gifts, plunging on any kind of crazy bet. The facts might not be straight but the colorful character is wholly captured and it is that enactment by Arnold that saves the film.

The Motion Picture Guide.

Thunder in the Night
Fox – 20 September 1935.
Directed by George Archainbaud and Produced by John Stone.

Cast: **Edmund Lowe** as Capt. Karl Torok, **Karen Morley** as Madalaine, **Paul Cavanagh** as Count Alvinczy, **Anders Van Haden** as a Policeman.

Reviews: Variety: 18 September 1925, p. 15.

Overly plotty murder mystery set in Budapest and starring Lowe as a clever police inspector out to stop a blackmailer who threatens to destroy the career of his friend, a newly appointed diplomat Cavanagh. When the blackmailer turns up dead, Cavanagh is under suspicion, so Lowe tries to clear his friend's name.

The Motion Picture Guide.

Anders Van Haden, the policeman in the center.
(Photo from the collection Constance J. Hurt, daughter of Myra Van Haden).

Barbary Coast
Goldwyn/UA - 27 September 1935.
Directed by Howard Hawks and Produced by Samuel Goldwyn.

Cast: **Miriam Hopkins** as Mary Rutledge, **Joel McCrea** as James Carmichael, **Edward G. Robinson** as Louis Chamalis, **Frank Craven** as Col. Marcus Aurelius Cobb, **Anders Van Haden** as McCready, 2nd Mate.

Reviews: NY Times: 14 October 1935, p. 21; Variety: 16 October 19, p. 22.

Note: An extremely short bit by Anders, McCready the 2nd Mate, in the beginning of this movie on the sailing ship approaching San Francisco.

A gaudy, tumultuous story, jammed with director Hawk's special action, this film rollicks with all the zest of 1850 San Francisco. Hopkins is a genteel lady from the East who finds her intended dead when arriving in the roughhouse city (at the time S.F. was a great, brawling seaport, the major American city on the Pacific; L.A. was only an adobe village to the south). Newspaper publisher Craven offers to take Hopkins in, but she refuses and is soon swept into the waterfront life of Robinson, crime czar of the city, becoming a plumed shill for his notoriously crooked roulette wheel, freely admitting that she is mercenary, only out for the percentage of gold she fleeces from gullible miners under her spell. Robinson is his typically snarling, wonderfully offensive self. He demands and gets Hopkins' affections but is snubbed by the town's upper crust. In one scene, while standing outside his sprawling saloon palace, the Bella Donna (writers Hecht and MacArthur though it funny to name the place after a deadly drug), Robinson waves to an official passing by with his wife in a carriage. They ignore him and Robinson explodes, telling Hopkins: "I'll fix him and that horse-face he calls his wife!" On a trip to the gold fields, Hopkins meets and falls in love with a young miner. On a visit to the Bella Donna, he loses all his money and takes a job as a dishwasher. Later, he and Hopkins attempt to flee the city, with Robinson in pursuit. The seemingly star-crossed lovers attempt to board a ship about to sail but Robinson stops them, shooting and wounding McCrea. Hopkins at her tearful, whining best, then begs Robinson to spare the young man, promising that if he does, she will stay with him and cherish his cruel affection. Realizing that she is truly in love with McCrea and rejecting her terms, Robinson blusters off, letting the pair escape, walking into the waiting arms of vigilantes who intend to hang him for the destruction of Craven's newspaper, which had tried to expose his shady operations. This was a vintage Hecht–McArthur script, full of wisecracks, sexual innuendoes and enough twists and turns to obscure the basic love triangle. The writers, who churned out the script in about a week of course concentrated on the evil character of Robinson, who embodies the soul of corruption. McCrea and Hopkins are skimpy by comparison, but the story rolls along like a roller coaster, crowded, noisy, full of teeming life.

The Motion Picture Guide.

The Affair of Susan
Universal - 7 October 1935.
Directed by Kurt Neumann and Produced by David Diamond.

Cast: **ZaSu Pitts** as Susan, **Dorothy Granger** as Girl in Candy Shop, **Anders Van Haden** as a Spieler.

Reviews: Variety: 6 November 1935, p. 20.

Slipshod slapstick story of two wallflowers who spend a day at Coney Island, meeting an assortment of dopey men and using up their time on whirlwind rides, with Pitts carrying most of the forced comedy. Well photographed, some good action and an above-average score by Waxman (music) can't save this one.

The Motion Picture Guide.

Desert Gold
Paramount - 30 March 1936.
Directed by James Hogan and Produced by Harold Hurley.

Cast: **Larry "Buster" Crabbe** as Moya, Indian Chief; **Robert Cummings** as Fordyce "Ford" Mortimer, **Marsha Hunt** as Jane Belding, **Tom Keene** as Dick Gale, **Monte Blue** as Chetley Kasedon, **Anders Van Haden** as an Indian Elder.

Reviews: Variety: 13 May 1936, p. 14.

Another version of Zane Grey's novel (Paramount did a whole series of superior Grey-based westerns in the early 1930's with Randolph Scott, directed by Henry Hathaway), this time starring Crabbe as chief of a small tribe of Indians who carefully guard the secrets of rich gold deposits in their territory. Blue and his gang of evil whites try to find a way to make the Indians talk. Meanwhile, Hunt is kidnapped by the gang. Crabbe rescues her and gets her back to her fiancé, Keene. Many of the best sequences are actually stock footage from earlier oaters directed by Hathaway.

The Motion Picture Guide.

Note: Anders Van Haden appears it the beginning of this movie in a night scene as an tribal elder with Chief Moya. He speaks the following lines: *"We are lost people in the world of the white man. We must adopt his cunning or perish." "It is lined with the feathers of the eagle." "The feathers are soft, they signify love."*

The Story of Louis Pasteur
Warner Bros. - 22 February 1936.
Directed by William Dieterle and Produced by Henry Blanke.

Cast: **Paul Muni** as Louis Pasteur, **Josephine Hutchinson** as Marie Pasteur, **Anita Louise** as Annette Pasteur, **Donald Woods** as Jean Martel, **Fritz Leiber** as Dr. Charbonnet, **Dickie Moore** as Phillip Meister, **Anders Van Haden** as a Laboratory Assistant.

Reviews: NY Times: 10 February 1936, p. 15; Variety: 12 February 1936, p. 16.

The film biography was a popular genre in the 1930s, and THE STORY OF LOUIS PASTEUR was one of the best despite Warner Bros. efforts to minimize the quality of the project. Muni (as Louis Pasteur) is working to find a cure for anthrax and hydrophobia. His colleagues at the Medical Academy are convinced his experiments are a waste of time, and Muni is ridiculed. He and his wife Hutchinson, along with their daughter Louise, decide to move into the French countryside, where Muni's experiments with sheep will be more readily accepted. Authorities learn that the sheep in Muni's area are disease-free, which causes some stir in the Medical Academy. Leiber, who has always been Muni's harshest critic, decides to rigidly test Muni's theory about microbes causing disease. Twenty-five sheep are given the anthrax vaccination while another 25 are left alone. Of course all the animals receiving the serum survive, and Muni is praised for his ground breaking work. Leiber remains obstinate, refusing to believe Muni's theories on microbes. Having found the cure for anthrax, Muni turns his attention toward the dread hydrophobia [rabies]. He creates a vaccine he believes will work, though the drug needs to be tested. Moore is a local child who is bitten by a mad dog. Muni takes his cure and vaccinates Moore. Meanwhile, Muni's daughter Louise is about to have her first child. Married to Muni's assistant Woods, Louise is in desperate need of a doctor to deliver her child. the only one available is Leiber, who remains at odds with Mini. He willingly agree to sterilize the tools needed to deliver Louise's baby if Muni will repudiate his rabies vaccination. Realizing this means life or death for his grandchild, Muni reluctantly gives in. Leiber appears to have had the last word with his blackmail, but much to his surprise Moore recovers after receiving Muni's vaccination. Leiber finally realizes that Muni's theories are correct, and

199

joins the Medical Academy in praising the doctor. THE STORY OF
LOUIS PASTEUR is well told, complemented by an intelligent script and
excellent performances. Careful attention is paid to scientific accuracy in
the film, with enough interesting characters to avoid becoming a preachy
educational film.

The Motion Picture Guide.

**Paul Muni and Josephine Hutchison in front with Anders Van Haden to
the left of her. (Photograph from the collection of Myra Van Haden).**

The Story of Louis Pasteur

Note: Anders appears in this video as a laboratory assistant and is seen several times in the basement laboratory of Louis Pasteur. His speaking part is as per the script below.

SEQUENCE 5 [of 12 sequences]

> MME. PASTEUR: Supper! (*Pasteur and his wife start toward the dining room.*)
> EXT. LABORATORY SHOWING STAIRWAY - MED. SHOT. *The veterinarian arrives and knocks on door. He carries a large, unwieldy cage containing a dog, and he has an air of mystery.*
> INT. LABORATORY-MED. SHOT. *An assistant hears the knock, another opens the door.*
> ASSISTANT [Anders Van Haden]: (*To others*) That's the veterinarian. Open the door!

Four-Star Scripts, 1936.

Anders Van Haden in the back, unidentified, Paul Muni, unidentified. (Photograph from the collection of Myra Van Haden).

The Witness Chair
RKO - 24 April 1936.
Directed by George Nichols, Jr.

Cast: **Ann Harding** as Paula Young, **Walter Abel** as James Trent, **Douglass Dumbrille** as Stanley Whittaker, **Frances Sage** as Constance Trent, **Paul Harvey** as Prosecuting Attorney Martin, **Anders Van Haden** as a Juror.

Reviews: NY Times: 18 April 1936; Syracuse Herald, 3 May 1936, p. 18.

Ann Harding's "Witness Chair" Ranks With Noted Trial Dramas

"The Witness Chair," starring Ann Harding, promises to take its place among such noted court-room drama successes as "Madame X" and "The Trial of Mary Dugan."

Miss Harding, incidentally, played the leading role in "The Trial of Mary Dugan," which enjoyed a phenomenal stage run throughout the United States and plays the Carolina Thursday.

Her splendid performance in the play caught the attention of motion picture producers and now after a prolonged success in Hollywod, she is again cast in a photoplay of similar theme to her outstanding stage triumph.

Adapted from a short novel by Rita Weiman which appeared in the Cosmopolitan magazine, "The Witness Chair" projects Miss Harding as the chief witness at a trial in which her lover is accused of a crime she committed forced by a sensational series of occurrences to let him stand trial, she finally comes forth with the truth in a drama-packed climax to save the defendant's daughter's reputation, and offset the proximity of a death for her lover demanded by the law.

Departing from the current trend in motion pictures, which offers a series of resplendent photographic backgrounds before film audiences, "The Witness Chair" has fewer settings than the average screenplay It relies on tense situations and excellent histrionics for its myriad moments of dramatic entertainment. Practically all fo the action takes place in a big city courtroom, but flashbacks denoting past action offer visual variety These contrasting locales include the office of a large corporaton, a business executive's private chamber and locations in na office building

DISTINGUISHED STAR

Shining light of many a pretentious screen production, Ann Harding now come sto the screen in "The Witness Chair", a tense murder trial drama produced by RKO Radio Pictures. Her supporting cast includes aWlter Abel, Douglass Dumbrille and Frances Sage.

Florence Morning News,
Sunday, May 24, 1936
(Permission to use granted by the Florence News)

ANDERS VAN HADEN

STATE OF CALIFORNIA
DIVISION OF REGISTRATION
DEPARTMENT OF MOTOR VEHICLES
RUSSEL. BEVANS, REGISTRAR OF VEHICLES

Operator's License

№ D310453

THIS CERTIFIES, *That* the person described and named below, was licensed on JUL 19 1935 to operate motor vehicles in accordance with provisions of the California Vehicle Act.

AGE 57 SEX male HEIGHT 6 ft
WEIGHT 180 COLOR EYES blue COLOR HAIR sandy

This License Expires JUL 19 1937 LS

William August Howell
1635 N Ogden Drive
Hollywood

OPERATOR MUST SIGN NAME WITH PEN AND INK ON LINE BELOW

Anders Van Haden's Drivers License.
Note that he still uses the name William August Howell.
(From the collection of Myra Van Haden).

Anders Van Haden and possibly an Auburn Roadster.
(Photo from the collection of Myra Van Haden).

RADIO BROADCASTS

The following are radio plays or broadcasts that William A. Howell (or Anders Van Haden or William Anders Howard) performed in from 1929 through 1936 in Hollywood and Los Angeles.

1933-1935 KFWB   CORONETS SERIES (English History)

1933-1935 KFWB   ITALIAN IDEALS (Borgia Family)

1929-1936 KFI   Various broadcasts

1929-1936 KNX   Various broadcasts

Videos and Internet

The following is a list of available DVD Videos and Internet links of the silent films and movies that Anders Van Haden or William A. Howell acted in or directed.

Jesus of Nazareth (1928)   DVD

Mamba (1930) (Reel 8)   DVD - www. youtube.com/ watch?v=Gg9pJtKeyA

Wir Schalten um auf Hollywood (1931)   DVD -

The Spider (1931)   DVD - www. youtube.com/watch?v= 9vzrVBYaaSs

The Yellow Ticket (1931)   DVD - www. youtube.com/watch?v= 0_ILYKCA66A

Ambassador Bill (1931)   VHS - https://ok.ru/video/284455930531

Surrender (1931)   DVD

Good Sport (1931)   DVD

Delicious (1931)   DVD - youtube.com/ playlist?list=PLvcg Vlg8yAH45dxoaE6cPkG-N8bHHHdHO

While Paris Sleeps (1932)   DVD - www.youtube.com/ watch?v=Vh36mRDhNEU

Rasputin and the Empress (1932)   DVD - (Warner Archive Collection)

A Passport to Hell (1932)   DVD - www. youtube.com/watch?v= 2jIboN-4nx4

The Fighting Marshall (1931)   DVD

The Match King (1932)   DVD - https://ok.ru/ video/270320929422

Cavalcade (1933)   DVD (20th Century Fox)

The Great Jasper (1933)   DVD

Secret of the Blue Room (1933)   DVD - www. youtube.com/watch?v= 9vzrVBYaaSs

Reunion in Vienna (1933)   DVD - (MGM)

Snug in the Jug (1934)	DVD - youtube.com/watch?v=D9Y2dNEHMFg
Riptide (1934)	DVD (MGM) - ok.ru/video/273243310734
Little Man, What Now? (1934)	DVD (Universal), VHS
Stamboul Quest (1934)	DVD
The World Moves On (1934)	DVD
We Live Again (1934)	DVD (MGM)
The County Chairman (1935)	DVD
Mystery Woman (1935)	DVD
The Florentine Dagger (1935)	DVD
Folies Bergére de Paris (1935)	DVD
Les Misérables (1935)	DVD (20th Century Fox)
The Bride of Frankenstein (1935)	DVD - (Universal)
Daring Young Man (1935)	DVD (20th Century Fox)
Diamond Jim (1935)	DVD - www.youtube.com/watch?v=RaP8f2pl0b0
Thunder in the Night (1935)	DVD (20th Century Fox)
Barbary Coast (1935)	DVD - (MGM)
Desert Gold (1936)	DVD - www.youtube.com/watch?v=wHUSID9i4tE
The Story of Louis Pasteur (1936)	www.youtube.com/watch?v=LptOXFYG_SI
The Witness Chair (1936)	DVD - (RKO)

Bibliography

I   Unpublished Material

Birth, Death, and Marriage Records. Personal Collection of Terris C. Howard.

Hurt, Constance J., *Unpublished photographs of Anders Van Haden*. Personal collection of Terris C. Howard (from Constance J. Hurt, December 1997).

The J. Willis Sayre-Carkeek Seattle Theatre Program Collection, *Programs 1884-1920, Volume 80, Moore Theatre 1909-1910, pages 9 & 10* (Courtesy of The Seattle Public Library, Art Department).

Van Haden, Myra, *Unpublished photographs, articles, stock tour schedules, 1908 diary, etc. of William A. Howell (AKA Anders Van Haden)*. Personal collection of Terris C. Howard (from Myra Van Haden, July 1974).

Van Haden, Myra, *Unpublished Scrapbooks given to Terris C. Howard, William D. Howard, Constance J. Hurt and Kathleen Howell (from Myra Van Haden, circa 1956)*.

Unpublished photographs of William A. Howell (AKA Anders Van Haden). Personal collections of Terris C. Howard, William D. Howard, Kathleen Howell, Constance J. Hurt and Myra Van Haden; Collections of The Academy of Arts and Sciences and University of California, Los Angeles.

II   Books - The following were used for research only.

Acker, Ally, *Reel Women* (Continuum Publishing Company: New York, 1991).

Alvarez, Max Joseph, *Index to Motion Pictures Review by VARIETY, 1907-1980* (The Scarecrow Press: Metuchen, NJ, 1982).

Baer, D. Richard, *The Film Buff's Checklist of Motion Pictures, 1912-1979* (Hollywood Film Archive: Hollywood, 1979).

Blum, Daniel, *A Pictorial History of the American Theatre, 1860-1976* (Crown Publishers: New York, 1977).

Boch, Hans-Michael, *Lexikon zum deutschsprachigen Film* (CineGraph: München, 1984).

Bowers, Q. David, *Thanhouser Films: An Encyclopedia and History* (Thanhouser Company Film Preservation, Inc, Scarecrow Press, Lanham, MD, Copyright©1997 - CD-ROM).

Bowser, Eileen, *The Transformation of Cinema, 1907-1915* (Charles Scribner's Sons: New York, 1990).

Bronner, Edwin J., *The Encyclopedia of the American Theatre, 1900-1975* (A.S. Barnes & Co: New York, 1980).

Brunas, Michael; John Brunas and Tom Weaver, *Universal Horrors* (McFarland and Co, Inc: Jefferson, NC, 1990).

Bucher, Felix, *Screen Series - Germany* (A.S. Barnes & Co: New York, 1970).

Connelly, Robert B., *The Motion Picture Guide, Silent Films, 1910-1936* (CineBooks, Inc: Chicago, 1986)

D'Agostino, Annette M., *An Index to Short and Feature Film Reviews in the Moving Picture World* (Greenwood Press: Westport, CT, 1995).

Durham, Weldon B., *American Theatre Companies, 1888-1930* (Greenwood Press: New York, 1987).

Eames, John Douglas, *The MGM Story, The Complete History of Fifty Roaring Years* (Crown Publishers: New York, 1975).

Everson, William K., *The Films of Laurel & Hardy* (The Citadel Press: New York, 1967).

Fernell, Gene, *American Film Studios: An Historical Encyclopedia* (McFarland & Company, Jefferson, NC, 1988).

Fetrow, Alan G., *Sound Films, 1927-1939, A United States Filmography* (McFarland & Company, Jefferson, NC, 1992).

Film Daily, *Annual Guide to Motion Picture Production - 1936* (The Film Daily: Hollywood, 1936).

Fisher, Kim N., *On the Screen* (Libraries Unlimited, Inc: Littleton, CO, 1986).

Graham, Cooper C. and Steven Higgins, eds. *D.W. Griffith and the Biograph Company* (The Scarecrow Press: Metuchen, NJ, 1985).

Halliwell, Leslie, *Halliwell's Filmgoer's Companion* (Charles Scribner's Sons: New York, 1984).

Hanson, Patricia King, *The American Film Institute Catalog, Vol F1, Feature Films, 1911-1920* (University of California Press: Berkeley, 1988).

Hanson, Patricia King, *The American Film Institute Catalog, Vol F3, Feature Films, 1931-1940* (University of California Press: Berkeley, 1993).

Hanson, Patricia King and Stephen L. Hanson, *Film Review Index, Vol 1: 1882-1949* (Oryx Press: Phoenix, Arizona, 1986).

Hartnell, Phyllis, *The Oxford Companion to the Theatre* (Oxford University Press: London, 1967).

Henderson, Robert M., *D.W. Griffith, His Life and Work* (Oxford University Press: New York, 1972).

Henderson, Robert M., *D.W. Griffith, The Years at Biograph* (Farrar, Straus and Giroux: New York, 1970).

Hirschhorn, Clive, *The Universal Story* (Crown Publishers: New York, 1983).

Hirschhorn, Clive, *The Warner Bros. Story* (Crown Publishers: New York, 1979).

Hobart, George V., *Experience, A Morality Play of Today* (The H.K. Fly Company: New York, 1915) - First Edition.

Hurst, Walter E. and William Storm Hale, *Film Superlist: 20,000 Motion Pictures in the U.S. Public Domain* (7 Arts Press: Hollywood, 1973).

Jesionowski, Joyce E., *Thinking in Pictures, Dramatic Structure in D.W. Griffith's Biograph Films* (University of California Press: Berkeley, 1987).

Jewell, Richard and Vernon Harbin, *The RKO Story* (Crown Publishers: New York, 1982).

Katz, Ephram, *The Film Encyclopedia* (Perigee Books/G.P. Putnam's Sons: New York, 1982).

Lee, Raymond, *The Films of Mary Pickford* (A.S. Barnes and Company: New York, 1970).

Library of Congress, *Motion Pictures, 1912-1939: Catalog of Copyright Entries* (Library of Congress:, Washington, 1951).

Library of Congress, *Newspapers in Microfilm* (Library of Congress: Washington, 1984).

Limbacher, James L., *Feature Films on 8mm and 16mm* (R.R. Bowker Company: New York, 1974).

Maltin, Leonard, *The Great Movie Shorts* (Bonanza Books: New York, 1972).

Maltin, Leonard, *The Laurel & Hardy Book* (Curtis Books: New York, 1973).

Maltin, Leonard, *Movie and Video Guide,* 1992 Edition (Penguin Books: New York, 1991).

Martin, Mick and Marsha Porter, *Video Movie Guide* (Ballantine Books: New York, 1991).

McCabe, John, *Laurel & Hardy* (E.P. Dutton: New York, 1975).

McNeil, Barbara and Miranda C. Herbert, *Performing Arts Biography Master Index,* Second Edition (Gale Research Co: Detroit, 1979).

Munden Kenneth W., *The American Film Institute Catalog, Vol F2, Feature Films, 1921-1930* (University of California Press: Berkeley, 1988).

Nash, James Robert and Stanley Ralph Ross, *The Motion Picture Guide, 1927-1983* (CineBooks, Inc: Chicago, 1985, 1986, 1987).

Nelson, Richard Alan, *Florida and the American Motion Picture Industry, 1898-1930* (Florida State University, 1980).

The New York Times, *Directory of the Film* (The New York Times, Arno Press/ Random House, 1971).

Noble, Lorraine, *Four-Star Scripts* (Doubleday, Doran & Company, Inc: Garden City, NY, 1936).

Nowlan, Robert A. and Gwendowlyn Wright Nolon, *Cinema Sequels and Remakes, 1903-1987* (McFarland & Co: Jefferson, NC, 1989).

Parish, James Robert and Michael R. Pitts, *Film Directors: A Guide to Their American Films* (The Scarecrow Press: Metuchen, NJ, 1974).

Pitts, Michael R., *Western Movies* (McFarland & Company: Jefferson, NC, 1986).

Quigley, Martin, Jr. and Richard Gertner, *Films in America,* 1929-1969 (Golden Press: New York, 1970).

Ragan, David, *Who's Who in Hollywood, 1900 - 1976* (Arlington House: New Rochelle, New York, 1976).

Riemann, Hugo Riemann, *Musik Lexikon: Erganzungsband* (B. Scholl Sohne: Mainz, 1972).

Samples, Gordon, *How to Locate Reviews of Plays and Films* (The Scarecrow Press, Inc: Metuchen, NJ, 1976).

Saechinger, Cesar, *International Who's Who in Music* (Current Literature Publishing Company: New York, 1918).

Scheuer, Steven H., *Movies on TV and Video Cassette 1991-1992* (Bantam Books: New York, 1990).

Shipman, David, *The Story of Cinema* (St. Martin's Press: New York, 1984).

Skretvedt, Randy, *Laurel and Hardy* (Moonstone Press: Beverly Hills, 1987).

Slide, Anthony, *The American Film Industry* (Greenwood Press: New York, 1986).

Slide, Anthony, *Aspects of American Film History Prior to 1920* (The Scarecrow Press: Metuchen, NJ, 1978).

Slide, Anthony, *International Film, Radio, and Television Journals* (Greenwood Press: Westport, Conn., 1985).

Slide, Anthony, *Early American Cinema* (The Scarecrow Press, Inc: Metuchen, NJ, 1994).

Smith, John M. and Tim Cawkwell, *The World Encyclopedia of the Film* (Galahad Books: New York, 1972).

Smith, Sharon, *Women Who Make Movies* (Hopkinson and Blake: New York, 1975).

Spehr, Paul C., *The Movies Begin* (The Newark Museum: Newark, NJ, 1977).

The Standard, June 1936 (Casting Directories Incorporated: Hollywood, 1936).

Stewart, John, *Filmarama, The Formidable Years, 1893-1919* (The Scarecrow Press: Metuchen, NJ, 1975).

Stewart, William T.; Arthur F. McClure and Ken D. Jones, *International Film Necrology* (Garland Publishing, Inc: New York, 1981).

Thomson, David, *A Biographical Dictionary of Film* (William Morrow and Co: New York, 1976).

Torrence, Bruce T., *Hollywood, The First Hundred Years* (New York Zoetrope: New York, 1982).

Truitt, Evelyn Mack, *Who was Who on Screen* (R.R. Bowker Co: New York, 1974, 1977, 1984).

Vinson, James, *Title Index* (St. James Press: Chicago, 1987).

Waldman, Harry, *Hollywood and the Foreign Touch, A Dictionary of Foreign Filmmakers and their Films from America* (The Scarecrow Press: Metuchen, NJ, 1994).

Weaver, John T., *Twenty Years of Silent, 1908 - 1928* (The Scarecrow Press: Metuchen, NJ, 1971).

Weiss, Ken and Ed Goodgold, *To Be Continued* (Crown Publishers Inc: New York, 1972).

III   Articles and Periodicals – The following were used for research only.

Moving Picture World (New York, 1907 to 1927).

New York Dramatic Mirror (New York, 1907 to 1914).

New York Times, The (New York, 1930 to 1936).

Seattle Post-Intelligencer, The (Seattle, 1910).

Seattle Times, The (Seattle, 1910).

Variety (New York, 1909 to 1936).

Printed in the United States
By Bookmasters